The Poems and Hymns of the New Testament

The Poems and Hymns
of the
New Testament

Philip Wesley Comfort

WIPF & STOCK · Eugene, Oregon

THE POEMS AND HYMNS OF THE NEW TESTAMENT

Copyright © 2010 Philip Wesley Comfort. All rights reserved. Except for brief quotations in critical publications or reviews, no part of this book may be reproduced in any manner without prior written permission from the publisher. Write: Permissions, Wipf and Stock Publishers, 199 W. 8th Ave., Suite 3, Eugene, OR 97401.

Wipf & Stock
An Imprint of Wipf and Stock Publishers
199 W. 8th Ave., Suite 3
Eugene, OR 97401

www.wipfandstock.com

ISBN 13: 978-1-60608-959-0

Manufactured in the U.S.A.

Contents

Introduction vii

1. The Gospel according to Matthew 1
2. The Gospel according to Mark 22
3. The Gospel according to Luke 25
4. The Gospel according to John 38
5. The Book of Acts 63
6. The Epistles of Paul 68
7. The Epistle to the Hebrews 94
8. The Epistle of James 99
9. The First Epistle of Peter 105
10. The First Epistle of John 109
11. The Epistle of Jude 122
12. The Book of Revelation 123

    Bibliography 142

Introduction

THE WORDS "BIBLE" AND "poetry" don't usually form a link in peoples' thinking. But poems from the Bible have been woven into the fabric of the English language. "The Lord is my shepherd, I shall not want" are the first two lines of a poem known as Psalm 23. The proclamation "they will beat their swords into ploughshares" (posted in front of the United Nations Building) comes from a line in Isaiah's poetry, as does the famous line, "the lion will lay down with a lamb" (see Isa 2:2; 11:6). Excerpts from Jesus' words are also cited without the speakers or writers thinking they are citing biblical poetry. In fact, many of Jesus' sayings have become part of our English language heritage. Just think of how many such statements have come just from Jesus' famous Sermon on the Mount. Who, for example, hasn't heard these statements used in common parlance: "you are the salt of the earth," "let your light shine before men," "don't store up treasures where moth and rust corrupts," "where your heart is, there is also your treasure," "no one can serve two masters," "seek and you will find/knock and the door will be opened."

The Bible is filled with poetry. One entire section of the Old Testament is comprised of poetic books—namely, Job, Psalms, Proverbs, Ecclesiastes, and Song of Songs. Many of the Prophets are also poetic: Lamentations (in its entirety), as well as large sections of Isaiah, Jeremiah, Ezekiel, Daniel, and the Minor Prophets. Anyone who opens a modern English translation and flips through the pages of the Old Testament will readily see that nearly half of it is poetry. While the New Testament cannot boast such abundance, it is not poetically impoverished. Large sections of Jesus' speeches are poetic—such as the Beatitudes, the Sermon on the Mount, and his final discourses in the book of John. The Epistles are also enriched with some excellent poems of the early Christians and of Paul, and the book of Revelation can boast of some outstanding hymns. When one reads the New Testament in the Greek text with an eye for poetry, many poetic passages spring to life, as well as a few hymns. These poems not only inform our minds, they stimulate our imaginations and arouse our emotions.

From the onset it must be said that it is sometimes difficult to distinguish between hymns and poems, because hymns are poems set to music—and we have no extant musical scores for any piece contained in the New Testament. (As far as I know, the earliest extant manuscript showing a Christian hymn with musical notation is found in P. Oxyrhynchus 1786, dated to the third century.) The only clues we are given in the New Testament is that sometimes the speakers are said to be singing, as in Revelation 5:9 and 15:3. Futhermore, it is not always easy to recognize what passage in the New Testament constitutes a poem. In English and many other languages, the appearance of the typeset on the page distinguishes poetry from prose, but the ancient Greek manuscripts did not have any poems set in any recognizable form on the page. Poetry was written as continuous text, just like prose. The way to differentiate poetry from prose is in the elevated style, rhythm, and uncommon words, as well as by the poetic conventions of meter, simile, metaphor, etc.

There are many poems in the Gospels, the majority of which can be attributed to Jesus. Whether Jesus spoke these originally in Greek or Aramaic (or both) is difficult to determine; it depends on the audience, whether it was all Jews (to whom he would have spoken in Aramaic) or a mixed audience (to whom he would have spoken in Greek—or, at least, would have had his message translated into Greek from Aramaic.) The Gospel writers Matthew and Luke were also poetic on occasion. John could also be poetic, not only in his Gospel, but also in his first Epistle and Revelation (which contains some hymns). Paul originated some poems, cited some early Christian hymns or poems, and recast several Old Testament passages in poetic pastiches. Peter and James display some poetic flare here and there, as did the writer of the epistle to the Hebrews. The New Testament also preserves some of the earliest Christian creeds, which were phrased as simple poetry (for the sake of memorization).

One of the purposes of this book is to help readers discover that Jesus was a prophetic poet. Most Bible readers wouldn't notice this about him because his speeches, as recorded in the Gospels, are almost always cast in a prose format, not poetry, in nearly all English translations. By contrast, much of the text of the Old Testament prophets is in poetic format. The prophets were excellent poets who delivered their addresses in rich and colorful verse—first orally and then in writing. Jesus, the premier prophet, often presented his message in powerful and memorable verse. In short, he was just as much a poet as were Isaiah, Jeremiah, Amos, and Hosea. In fact, his poetry was informed and inspired by theirs—he often recited their verse or alluded to it. Jesus startled his audience, not only with God-inspired truth, but often with refreshingly new poetry.

The prophets' poetic verse was designed to attract the attention of the audience. If the presentation was blandly prosaic, their audiences would not be allured or impressed. In the same manner, Jesus' teachings were extremely attractive, not only because of the truths he shared, but because his language was often colorfully poetic. The poetic quality of Jesus' sayings aided in their memorization. His poems, along with his parables (of which he was a master), became the substance of the Jesus *Logia* that was passed on from the apostles to other Christians, first by word of mouth and then in writing.

Jesus' poetry often came in the form of short aphorisms—two-liners, such as in the following: "foxes have holes, birds have nests,/but the Son of Man has nowhere to lay his head." But there are longer poetic passages in the Gospels, which his disciples committed to memory and then later translated from Aramaic to Greek (unless, of course, Jesus originally spoke these poems in Greek). The Beatitudes is a sublime example of a substantial poem, as are many others which are presented in this volume.

It is also possible that Jesus himself wrote these poems, along with other *logia*, or dictated them to one of his disciples functioning as an amanuensis. If this conjecture has any validity, the disciples would not have had to commit Jesus' words to memory, preserve them through an oral tradition, and then write them down. Rather, they could have gotten them straight from Jesus' pen or mouth. Admittedly, this is a revolutionary idea because we don't usually think of Jesus as being a writer or author. But why couldn't Jesus, for example, write out the text that is known as the Sermon on the Mount or at least dictated it to one of his disciples, such as Matthew. This disciple, as a tax collector, would have been handy with a pen and could have easily taken down dictation from Jesus, much as Silas took down dictation from Peter to write 1 Peter (5:12) or Tertius took down dictation from Paul (Rom 16:22) to write the epistle known as Romans.

Regardless of who wrote the *logia* in the Gospels, there is diversity of opinion about which Gospel texts are poetic or which are prose. Few would deny that the Beatitudes are poetry. They are set as such in Greek texts and English versions. Few would also deny the poetic quality of the traditional Lord's Prayer in Matthew 6, as well as for the longer Lord's Prayer in John 17. Though some might call these portions exalted prose, I see them as poetry because these writings have cadence, lexical beauty, and lyrical texture. The translators of the New Jerusalem Bible saw nearly all of Jesus' monologues in the Gospel of John as deserving a poetic format—much like that found in the Old Testament Prophets. The New English Bible and Moffatt's translation also present some of Jesus' passages as poems. But they do so sporadically.

There would also be a diversity of opinion about other passages from Acts to Revelation. However, I think we can recognize several kinds of poems and some hymns in these books. Several are renditions of Old Testament passages, often taken from the Septuagint. Many of the Greek translators who participated in the production of the Septuagint were creative poets in their own right; they did not merely render the Hebrew word for word, but translated according to the principle of dynamic equivalence. Paul frequently strung together several of passages of the Septuagint in a poetic pastiche. Peter did the same in his first epistle. A few xii *The Poems and Hymns of the New Testament*

of the poems in Paul's Epistles are early Christian creeds, some of which may have been hymns (as in 1 Tim 2:5–6; 3:16). Most of the poems are original creations of the New Testament writers themselves. A few of Paul's poems are presented in the form of prayer (as in Eph 1 and 3). In this, they model prayers in the Old Testament such as the one found in 2 Chronicles 6:40–41 (see also Neh 9:5–37).

The portions I have presented as poetry are often treated as such in the standard Greek New Testament, *Novum Testamentum Graece* (Nestle-Aland 27th edition = NA[27]). Although this edition has the same text as the *Greek New Testament* (United Bible Societies 4th edition), one notable difference is that *Novum Testamentum* has far more passages presented in poetic format. (Both editions usually present Old Testament quotations in the New Testament as poems, but NA[27] exceeds this by typesetting several passages in poetic format.) In this volume I have presented far more passages as poems than are found in *Novum Testamentum Graece*, as well as in standard English versions. If one excludes the citation of Old Testament passages in the New Testament (which are set as poetry), most English versions present only a handful of poems. The New Jerusalem Bible has the most poetry, especially in John's Gospel and 1 John. I do not think the Gospel has as much poetry as the translators of the New Jerusalem Bible present, but I have followed the lead of the New Jerusalem Bible in presenting the entire epistle of 1 John in poetic format. I exceed the New Jerusalem Bible, however, in recognizing many poetic passages in the New Testament epistles.

In my English translation of the poems in this volume I have attempted to follow the model known as functional equivalence—or what I would call "poetic equivalence." This

Introduction xiii

means that I have produced these poems as modern English poetry. As such, I have not been bound to slavishly follow the bi-colon pattern that is often found in Hebrew poetry and carried over into the Greek New Testament. However, I have tried to be sensitive to the echoing effect created by the parallelism in the two clauses. Furthermore, I have not sought to make these poems fit a set meter. And I have not attempted to systematically rhyme, which is also the case with Greek poetry. Rather, the poems are natural expressions seeking to convey the sense of the Greek in a way that is consistent with modern English poetry.

THE GOSPEL OF MATTHEW

Matthew preserved one passage of John the Baptit's poetic voice: "The Baptism of Jesus and the Baptism of John" (3:7–12). Matthew also has two poems that are adapted from Old Testament texts: (1) "Jesus, Light for the Nations" (4:15–16), Matthew's own translation of the Hebrew text of Isaiah 9:1–2, and (2) "Jesus, the Chosen Servant" (12:18–21), also Matthew's own translation of Isaiah 41:1–4, borrowing somewhat from the Septuagint.

The rest of the poems, of which there are 18, originated with Jesus. Of course, since Matthew was the one who put them in written form, he had some influence on the final text. In two of Jesus' poems, he wove passages from the Old Testament into his composition. In "Jesus' Message for John the Baptist" (11:1–19), he used Malachi 3:1 in verse 10, with some of his own alterations (see poem for details). For verses 14–15 in the poem "The Reason for Parables" (13:10–17), he used Isaiah 6:9–10 in the form it appears in the Septuagint. Isaiah 6:9–10 is the most quoted Old Testament text in the

New Testament (Matt 13:14–15; Mark 4:11–12; Luke 8:10; John 12:40; Acts 28:26–27; Rom 11:8) because it provides a perfect prophetic explanation for Israel's non-receptivity of Jesus as the Messiah.

Concerning the other 16 poems, half of them appear in the Sermon on the Mount (chpts. 5–7). This sermon, likely a composite of various messages Jesus gave throughout his ministry, is jeweled with several sparkling poems. The pearl among them is the Beatitudes (5:3–11). The poem has a uniform syntactical structure, lyrical cadence, and eschatological promises packed with mystery and ambiguity. This is why the poem is both so memorable and ponderable. Many of the alluring statements, such as "the meek inherit the earth," "the pure in heart see God," and "the poor in spirit possess the kingdom," are not easily explainable. What is it to be meek, to be pure in heart, to be poor in spirit? And what does it mean to inherit the earth or see God? These mysteries, which push the reader beyond certain horizon, are the marks of good poetry.

THE GOSPEL OF MARK

Among the Gospels, Mark's Gospel has the fewest poems for two reasons. First, the writer, John Mark, was primarily focused on providing a narrative of Jesus' accomplishments moreso than a record of Jesus' speeches. Whereas the other three Gospels have lengthy portions of Jesus' speeches, Mark has very few—chapter 13 (Jesus' discourse on the eschaton) is the most substantial. Second, the other two Synoptic Gospels (Matthew and Luke) often have the same portions of Jesus' speech as are recorded in Mark, but with more text. For that reason, I more frequently translated the pericope from Matthew and/or Luke than from Mark. In addition to the short poetic prologue to Mark (which weaves in two OT texts), Mark has one distinct passage, which I call "Severe Discipleship" (9:42–50).

THE GOSPEL OF LUKE

Luke, a Gentile physician, was skilled with the Greek language. This is evident in his lexical range and complex syntax, as well as in his rhythmical poetry. His most famous poems are "The Annunciation" (1:30–33, 35), "The Magnificat" (1:46–55), "The Benedictus" (1:67–79), and "The Nunc Dimitis" (2:28–32). These poems show that he had adapted the Hebrew language to Greek poetry in a rich blend of authenticity (as concerning the original speakers of these poems—Gabriel, Mary, Zechariah, Simeon) and original creativity (on Luke's part). The other poems in Luke, all spoken by Jesus, reveal the same fertile mixture.

Several of the poems in Matthew could have also been placed with Luke because they are synoptic passages. However, I chose to do more of these in Matthew because usually the Matthew pericope had more text than in the Luke parallel. Such is not the case, however, in Luke's version of Jesus' famous sermon, which includes "woes" (or "miseries"), as well as blessings (6:20–21, 24–25), and in the poems called "The Eye, the Body's Lamp" (11:33–36), "Signs of his Coming" (12:49–56), and "Camel through a Needle's Eye" (18:23–24). So these are included in the Luke section.

THE GOSPEL OF JOHN

John was a poet; his Gospel, an elaborate poem of sorts. John specialized in double meaning, allusion, allegory, irony, and symbolism. His well-crafted work, like a symphony, advances new themes, drifts into others, then returns with similar sounds yet fresh and alluring.

John's Gospel is replete with poetry, as can be evidenced in the New Jerusalem Bible, which has nearly all of the Gospel in poetic format. Though I do not consider the Gospel to have as much poetry as is seen in the New Jerusalem Bible, I recognize that this Gospel is quite poetic. Some of the most elevated poetry is seen in the prologue (1:1–18), a masterpiece among New Testament prologues, as well as in Jesus' magnificent monologues in chapters 5–8, and his upper room discourse (chpts. 14–16), which is capped with a sublime prayer (chpt. 17).

Like a clear deep lake, John's poetic style is deceptively simple in terms of vocabulary (some of the simplest in the New Testament) yet profoundly deep with respect to theological thought. The poetry of Jesus, as presented by John, is mystically alluring; it calls the reader to explore various levels of meaning. The Greek is often polyvalent—one word or one phrase exuding several denotations. For example, in John 3:8 the noun *pneuma* with the verb *pnei* convey three levels of meaning at the same time: "the wind/spirit/breath... blows/spirits/breathes." Needless to say, this is difficult, if not impossible, to duplicate in English, though I have tried my best. Various notes here and there will help the reader understand the polyvalence.

THE BOOK OF ACTS

This historical narrative of the early church does not have as much poetry as one sees in Luke's previous work, his Gospel. There are a few Old Testament poetic passages pertaining to fulfilled messianic prophecy—passages that were important to the early church's understanding of Jesus' mission, as well as their own (see "The Name of the Lord Saves"; "Jesus, the Risen One"; "Jesus the Silent Lamb": and "Gentiles Will Seek the Lord"). One remarkably original poem, quite Hellenistic in character, is one found in Acts 17, which preserves a portion of Paul's speech at the Aeropagus. In this speech, Paul waxes eloquent, citing the lines of two poets (Epimenides and Aaratus) within the context of his own poetic presentation (see notes on Acts 17).

THE EPISTLES OF PAUL

The poems in Paul's Epistles can be placed in four categories: (1) original creations, (2) renditions of Old Testament passages as single pericopes and renditions of pastiches (a stringing together of various Old Testament passages with some original additions and/or changes); (3) recitations of early Christian creeds; (4) recitations of early Christian "sayings." Paul also recited some early Christian hymns, some of which are probably one in the same as the early Christian creeds (see 1 Tim 2:5-6; 3:16; 2 Tim 1:8-10).

Among Paul's original creations, the most brilliant poems are "Encomium to Christ's Love" (Rom 8:28-39); "the Supremacy of Love" (1 Cor 13); "the Incarnation of Christ" (Phil 2:5-11); "the Preeminent Christ" (Col 1:14-20). There are two sublime poetic prayers in Ephesians: "Prayer for Enlightening and Empowering" (1:15-23), and "Prayer for Experiencing Christ's Indwelling" (3:14-21). Both of these prayers are carefully crafted poems.

Paul's recitations of Old Testament passages often came from memory; they are rarely verbatim quotations.

In general he preferred to use the Septuagint as his source, which he often adjusted for the sake of his particular use. In Romans, however, he took the time to look up the Old Testament verses. Nearly all of these verses have to do with Israel's rejection of Jesus as the Messiah and God's election of the Gentiles. These verses became fundamental to Paul's mission of taking the gospel to the Gentiles. On occassion, he patched together several snippets of Old Testament texts in interesting pastiches. Paul's Epistle to the Romans contains two noteworthy collages: "Promises for the Gentiles and Jews" (9:24–33) and "The Root of Jesse for the Gentiles" (15:8–13). (See notes on these poems.)

In Paul's writings we also find several early Christian creeds, which were confessions (or professions) of allegiance to the core doctrines of the Christian faith. The "Creed of Monothesism" (1 Cor 8:6) is a kind of Christian shema; the "Creed of Christian Unity" (Eph 4:4–6) proclaims the essentials of what all Christians should believe; the "Creed of Christ, the Mediator" (1 Tim 2:5–6) affirms Christ's role of Savior and perpetual mediator between God and humans; the "Creed of the Mystery of Godliness" (1 Tim 3:16) lauds the mystery of Christ's life on earth—from incarnation to ascension.

The Pastoral Epistles (which I consider to be part of the Pauline collection of writings) contain five "trustworthy sayings," which are sayings from early church tradition pertaining to matters of salvation (1 Tim 1:15; 3:1; 4:9–10; 2 Tim 2:10–13; Titus 3:4–8). Just as the Gospel writers passed on Christ's "sayings" (the *Logia*), so Paul passed on to Timothy and Titus some of the sayings of the early Christians. We are not sure if Paul cited the entire sayings or just parts, and we do not know if Paul altered these sayings for his specific adaptions. In any event, two of these sayings have enough text to demonstrate they were poetic passages: the "Saying of Faithfulness" (2 Tim 2:10–13) extols faithfulness to Christ no matter what suffering it brings; and "the Saying of the Savior's Epiphany" (Titus 3:4–8) is a well-crafted poem celebrating the benefits the believers have because of the Savior's epiphany.

THE EPISTLE TO THE HEBREWS

The author of the Epistle to the Hebrews was quite eloquent. Many commentators have presumed the writer to have been Apollos, who was an Alexandrian Jewish Christian trained in rhetoric and symbolism. This epistle, written in the form of a sermon, has elevated prose throughout, sprinkled with a few poetic passages. The prologue (1:1–4) is a magnificent poem in and of itself; yet this prologue is preamble to the entire first chapter, which could be considered a larger prologue—set in the form of a pastiche with interspersed commentary introducing the theme of Jesus' superiority to all the angels because he is the enthroned Son of God. The sermon continues on the larger theme of Jesus' superiority to everything held dear by Jews: Moses, Aaron, the high priesthood, the atoning sacrifice, and the covenant. Jesus is the superior messenger (1:5–2:18), apostle (3:1–4:13), and high priest (4:14–7:28), with a better covenant (8:1–9:28), better sacrifice (10:1–39), offering faith as the better way (11:1–12:29). The thrust of the sermon is to convince Jewish Christians to let go of their Jewish ways (especially with respect to the Temple sacrifices) and embrace the superior Christ. Sometimes the author uses Old Testament poetic passages to underscore his message—especially with respect to the new covenant (Jer 31:31–34); other times he adapts some Old Testament passages for his own purposes, as in "Christ Incarnate for Sacrice" (Heb 10:4–7, taken from Ps 40:6–8); still other times he offers fresh poems, as in "the Panegyric" (Heb 12:18–24) and final doxology (13:20–21).

THE EPISTLES OF JAMES, 1 PETER, AND JUDE

The letter of James was written like a collection of wise Jewish teachings, much like Jesus' Sermon on the Mount (Matt 5–7). There are striking similarities in language and style between this epistle and Jesus' sermon (cf. James 1:2 with Matt 5:11; 1:5 with 7:7; 1:16–17 with 7:11; 1:22–25 with 7:24–27; 2:12–13 with 6:14–15; 3:6 with 5:22; 3:12 with 7:16; 4:4 with 6:24; 5:1–6 with 6:19–21).

Peter's first epistle has a few noteworthy poems, each of which is built around poetic Old Testament passages. Peter—or should I say, his writer Silvanus (1 Peter 5:13) —crafted three excellent poems that celebrate Christ, as (1) the Regenerator, (2) the Suffering Healer, and (3) the Cornerstone. These poems build off Old Testament passages that are interpreted Christo-centrically.

It is most likely that Silvanus (also known as Silas) was the writer of this epistle. His name appears at the end of 1 Peter (5:12), where the text explicitly states that Peter wrote the epistle "through Silvanus." This means that Silvanus either functioned as an amanuensis for Peter, or translated Peter's letter (from Aramaic to Greek) as Peter dictated it, or composed a letter based on Peter's thoughts. The last mentioned function was not an unusual practice in ancient times or in modern. Certain people, not gifted with writing, give that task to another, who puts down in words the thoughts of the author. (In modern times, this person is often called "the ghost writer.") Of all the options, it seems most likely that Silvanus composed the letter based on Peter's thoughts. Peter, a Galilean fisherman, would probably not have had the ability to write the kind of Greek we see in this epistle.

Silvanus (Silas) was a leading Christian in the church at Jerusalem; he was a prophet and he was a Roman citizen. He was one of the two men (along with Judas Barsabbas) chosen by the church to write the letter of the Jerusalem Council to Antioch and deliver it to the Gentile churches in Antioch, Syria, and Cilicia (Acts 15:22–23). The Greek of Acts 15:23 (*grapsantes dia cheiros auton*:"having written it with their hands") refers to "two of the church leaders—Judas (also called Barsabbas) and Silas" in the previous verse (15:22). It was customary in ancient times for the composer or composers of an epistle to also be the reader or readers of that epistle. Thus, Silas and Judas Barsabbas were the two who wrote the letter and read the letter to the church in Antioch (Acts 15:30–31).

THE FIRST EPISTLE OF JOHN

John's first Epistle, with its spiraling repetition of themes, is sublimely symphonic. It is worthy of being read as poetry. (The New Jerusalem Bible presents the entire epistle as a poem.) The following arrangement, which differs from that of the New Jerusalem Bible, demonstrates this spiraling repetition: with the pattern of A B C, A B C, B C A.

> Prologue (1:1–4)
> A1. Living Righteously in Light & Truth (1:5–2:6)
> B1. Living in Light & Love (2:7–17)
> C1. Knowing False Teaching & True (2:18–27)

A2. Living Righteously in the Truth (2:28–3:10)
B2. Living in Love (3:11–24)
C2. Knowing False Teaching & True (4:1–6)
B3. Living in Love (4:7–5:4)
C3. Knowing False Teaching & True (5:5–13)
A3. Living Righteously in the Truth (5:14–21)

THE BOOK OF REVELATION

Of all the books of the New Testament, Revelation is most like the Old Testament Prophets (especially Ezekiel and Daniel). As with these books, Revelation contains several poems of various types. The book begins with a powerfully poetic prologue and then presents the reader with several more poems, which are often in the form of chants or hymns sung by celestial beings: angels, four living creatures (zoa), the 24 elders, and saints in heaven. These paeans are exultant praises to God for his creation and judgment, as well as to Jesus Christ for his sacrificial role in redemption and kingly role in the coming kingdom.

The poems and hymns in Revelation have the look of being carefully composed, especially in contrast to other portions where John appears to have written down the visions as he saw them. From the statement in Revelation 10:4 (where John sees a vision, is about to write it down, but then is told by a voice in heaven: "seal up what the seven thunders have said, and do not write it down"), we can imagine that John recorded the revelations as he saw them. These portions often have unfixed grammatical errors (see Comfort's *New Testament Text and Translation Commentary* on Rev 1:15; 2:20a; 10:7; 14:19; 16:4) and asynedon (as in 7:13). By contrast, the poems and hymns display balance and structure, with a touch of continuity from one poem to another via the repetition of various phrases such as "him who is, who was, and who is to come." Of course, it is possible that John recorded the hymns and chants as he heard them (repeated as they were over and over), but it is more likely that he edited them to give them form and unity.

In a sense the entire book could be considered poetic inasmuch as John repeatedly used similes to describe what he saw and heard ("it looked like," "it sounded like," etc.). But I have selected various portions which appear to be poetic units in and of themselves.

1

The Gospel according to Matthew

The Baptism of John and the Baptism of Jesus (3:7–12)

7 Seeing many Pharisees and Sadducees coming
to observe John's baptism, he rebuked them:

You brood of vipers, snaking your way here to see me.
Have you been warned to flee God's imminent anger?
8 You need to produce the fruit of genuine change.
9 Do not deceive yourselves by thinking,
"we have Abraham as our father."

God is able to raise up his children
from these very stones I'm standing on.
10 Even now the axe is ready to cut the roots
of every tree that doesn't produce good fruits.
They will be cut down and thrown into the fire.

11 I baptize with water, expecting you to change,
but the coming One is more potent than me
(I am not even worthy to carry his sandals);
he will baptize you with the fire of the sacred Spirit.
12 The winnow in his hand threshes the chaff,
which is blown away into an unquenchable fire.
Then he will he gather the wheat into his granary.

This passage is poetic by virtue of its colorful images. John the Baptist spoke like one of the OT prophets (especially see Mic 4:12), using an array of geographical images (snakes, rocks, water, fire) and agricultural images (fruit trees, threshing, winnowing, wheat, granary) to present a God who is looking for lives to change and be spiritually productive or suffer the consequences.

Jesus, Light for the Nations (4:15–16)

> 15 *It happened in the land of Zebulun and Naphtali,*
> *on the road by the sea,*
> *across the Jordan, in Galilee of the Gentiles:*
> 16 *the people sitting in darkness*
> *saw[1] a magnificent light,*
> *which dawned on those living*
> *under the shadow of death.*

Poems from the Sermon on the Mount

The Beatitudes (5:3–12)

> 3 Those with impoverished spirits are blessed,
>   for they will be enriched in God's kingdom.
> 4 Those who mourn are blessed,
>   for I have come to comfort them.
> 5 Those who live in meekness are blessed,
>   for I promise them a new earth.
> 6 Those who hunger and thirst for justice are blessed,
>   for they will be satisfied when it comes.

---

1. In Matthew's rendition of the OT text (Isa 9:1–2), he changes the future tense "will see" to "saw" and "the light will shine" to "the light has dawned" because he saw the prophecies fulfilled in Jesus' epiphany.

7 Those who show mercy to others are blessed,
>   for mercy will return to them.
8 Those with transparent hearts are blessed,
>   for they will see nothing else but God.
9 Those who live as peacemakers are blessed,
>   for they will be known as children of God.
10 Those who are persecuted for the sake of justice are blessed,
>   for they will find refuge in the kingdom.

11 Blessings to you who are reviled, persecuted, and maligned because of your allegiance to me.
12 May joy come to you as the kingdom's rich reward,
>   for so were the prophets persecuted before you.

This passage is the first example of Jesus' poetic power. The poem is thought-provoking in that it overturns traditional values. The Beatitudes (Latin for "blessings") are universally recognized in modern English translations as poetry (so also the standard Greek NT editions). The rhythm, syntactical structure, and lexical beauty in the Greek call for the same in English. Even literal translations can't help but be poetic. In my translation, I have sought to expand some of the images so as to offer a fresh look. I have, however, kept the traditional rendering "are blessed" (a divine passive) because I feel there is no other English word that does *makarios* justice in this context. (In the Greek, the word is placed first in the first line of every cola, whereas I have placed it last. Both placements signal emphasis.) The expressions "are happy" or "are fortunate" are too light to convey the notion of spiritual contentment.

Salt and Light (5:13–16)

> 13 You are the salt of the earth;
> > but if salt becomes insipid, how can it be recovered?
> > It is no longer good for anything
> > but to be thrown out and stomped into the ground.
>
> 14 You are the light of the world.
> > A city situated on a mountain cannot be hid.
> 15 No one lights an oil lamp to put it under a basket,
> > but on a lampstand, where it illumines everyone in the house.
> 16 So also, let your light glow in the presence of others
> > so they may notice your good works and praise the heavenly Father.

I am not sure if these two poems belong together or if each was a separate Jesus "saying" attached here by Matthew. Mark (9:50) and Luke (14:34) have a similar saying about salt unattached to the saying about light. The connecting theme in Matthew is that of effectiveness. Salt is a preservative and that which gives zest to food; salt (as used in a covenant of salt; Num 18:19; 2 Chr 13:5) also speaks of being a sign of peace-making (see Mark 9:50). Those who are the salt of the earth give life and peace to others. The image of the light doesn't need comment.

The Lord's Prayer (6:9–13)

> 9 Our Father, who inhabits heaven,
> > your Name alone is sacred.
> 10 May you kingdom earth with heaven
> > and fulfill your heart's desire.

11 Give us today the sustaining bread,
12 and forgive us our debts,
 as we also have forgiven our debtors.
13 Don't lead us down temptation's path;
 from every evil rescue us.[2]

Storing Treasure (6:19–21)

19 Do not amass earthly possessions
 which moths eat, rust corrodes,
 and robbers plunge and steal.
20 Store up heavenly treasures
 which neither moth nor rust devours
 and thieves can't ever rob.
21 Your treasures are your heart's desires.

The syntactical and lexical presentation of the first two verses in Greek is a work of beautiful symmetry, which I have attempted to imitate in English (while allowing for some verbal variation). Moth, rust, and thieves are the earthly robbers of all treasures, but they cannot touch what has been treasured in heaven.

Two Lords: God and Money (6:24–29, 31–34)

24 No one can serve two lords;
 you will either hate one and love the other,
 or be devoted to one and despise the other.
You cannot serve both God and Money.

---

2. Several of the earliest manuscripts (ℵ B D Z) end here. Other manuscripts give evidence of several additions made by various scribes (L W Q Maj—so Textus Receptus and KJV). The most well-known addition is "For yours is the kingdom, the power, and the glory forever, amen." (For more on this, see my book, *New Testament Text and Translation Commentary*, 15–16).

25 Do not worry about your life,
   what you will eat or how you will clothe your body.
Isn't life more than food,
   and your body more than clothes?
26 Look at the birds in the sky;
   they neither sow nor reap nor harvest,
   yet your heavenly Father feeds them.
Aren't you valued more than they?

27 Who among you, by being anxious,
   can add a single hour to your life-span?[3]

28 Why do you worry about clothes?
   Consider the lilies of the field;
   they do not card[4] or spin or labor,
29 yet even Solomon in all his splendor
   was not clothed like one of these.

30 If God so dresses the field with flowers,
   which live today and are burned tomorrow,
   will he not clothe you so much better?
   Where is your faith?
32 Nations the world over strive to obtain all these things.
   Since your heavenly Father knows all you need,
33 seek his kingdom first and his justice,
   and all these things will come your way.

34 Do not be anxious about tomorrow,
   for tomorrow will have its own anxieties.
Each day has enough trouble of its own.

---

3. Or, "add one inch to your height."

4. "they do not card" (*ou xenousin*) is the reading of two early manuscripts: ℵ and P. Oxyrhynchus 655. All other manuscripts read "they grow" (*auxanousin*), which is likely a scribal misreading of *ou xenousin*.

In this poem, which includes 7 aphorisms (each stanza but the penultimate), Jesus turns his audience's attention to God's providential care as expressed through nature (birds, lilies, grasses of the field). This same God, who is concerned for people's lives, should be trusted, not the god known as Money ("Mammon" in the Greek).

Gift-giving (7:6–12)

6 Do not give sacred things to dogs;
    and don't throw your pearls to wild pigs,
or they will trample them, turn on you, and tear you to pieces.

7 Ask and it will be given you;
    search and you will find;
knock and the door will be opened to you.

8 For everyone who asks receives,
    and everyone who searches finds,
and the door opens for everyone who knocks.

9 Is there anyone who would give his son a stone
    if he asked for bread?
10 Or would give him a snake
    if he asked for fish?

11 If even bad people give good gifts to their children,
    how much more will the heavenly Father
    give good things to those who ask him!

12 Do for others what you wished they would do for you.
This is the essence of the sacred Writings.[5]

---

5. Lit., "the Law and the Prophets," an idiom for the Jew's sacred Scriptures.

I think 7:6 (first stanza) and 7:12 (last stanza) bracket 7:7–11 (the four stanzas in between) because all these "sayings" (or aphorisms) pertain to giving and receiving. Other readers may want to limit the poem to 7:7–11. Either way, there is remarkable symmetry and poetic balance throughout. Jesus' use of hyperbole ("stone for bread" and "snake for fish") is what makes Jesus' speech both poetic and appealing to his audience.

Two Gates (7:13–14)

> 13 Enter through the narrow gate;
> for the gate and road to destruction are wide open,
> > and there are many who walk this way.
> 14 The gate is tight and the road is narrow leading to life,
> > and there are few who find it.

The power of this poem is in its simple yet poignant imagery: two gates and two roads, leading either to eternal life or destruction, and two kinds of travelers: the "many" on the path to destruction; the "few" on the path to life.

Good Fruit and Bad (7:15–20)

> 15 Beware of false prophets,
> > who come to you in sheep's clothes,
> > but really are ravenous wolves.

> 16 You will recognize them by their fruits.

> Are grapes gathered from thorns,
> > or figs from thistles?
> 17 Every good tree grows good fruit,
> > but the bad tree grows bad fruit.

18 A good tree cannot produce unhealthy fruit,
>   nor can an unhealthy tree produce good fruit.
19 Every tree not growing good fruit
>   is cut down and thrown into the fire.

20 You will recognize them by their fruits.

The imagery in this poem is startling in that false prophets are depicted as wolves in sheep's clothes, which is immediately followed by an organic aphorism: "you will recognize them by their fruits," which is then, more naturally, repeated at the end of the poem. Parts of this poem have been sown into the fabric of the English language. What English-speaking adult doesn't know what this means: "Beware of false prophets in sheep's clothes; they are really ravenous wolves"; or what this means: "you will know them by their fruits"? Jesus' poetry is more engrained in the English language than we often recognize.

The New and Old (9:15–17)

15 The bridegroom's friends shouldn't mourn
>   but enjoy the pleasure of being with him.
The days will come, after the bridegroom leaves them,
>   that they will experience deprivation.

16 No one sews a piece of new, unshrunk cloth onto an old garment,
>   because the piece will pull on it and make a bigger tear.

17 Neither is new wine poured into old wineskins,
>   because the wine will spill when the wineskins burst.
New wine is poured into fresh wineskins,
>   so that both can be preserved.

This passage is called a "parable" in a parallel passage (Luke 5:36–38). The Greek word *parabole* means "a comparison" and can denote simply figurative language (see BAGD, 612). Most of Jesus' parables are easily recognizable beause they come in story form or are preceded with words announcing a simile such as "the kingdom is like . . ." In this poem, there is no story and it is not a simile. So, I take it to be figurative language, hence a poem. Jesus' disciples were enjoying the newness of being with Jesus whose "new way" was disappointing traditional religious expectations (by not fasting, etc.). The message of the poem is that the new cannot live with the old.

The Cost of Discipleship (10:24–42)

24 A disciple is not superior to his teacher,
    nor a servant above his master;
25 the best a disciple can do is become like his teacher,
    and the servant like his master.
If they have called the master of the house "Beelzeboul,"[6]
how much more will they malign those of his household!
26 But have no fear of them.

There is nothing veiled that will not be unveiled,
    and nothing hidden that will not become revealed.
27 What I say to you in the dark,
    speak in the light;
and what you hear me whisper
    broadcast from the housetops.

---

6. "Beelzeboul" is a surrogate for Satan.

28 Don't dread those who kill the body but can't kill the soul;
>   fear him who can annihilate both soul and body in hell.[7]

29 Are not two sparrows sold for a penny?
>   Yet not one of them falls to the ground
>   without your Father knowing it.
30 Every hair on your head has been counted.
31 Don't be troubled; you are valued more than sparrows.

32 Everyone who confesses me in the presence of others
>   will be acknowledged by me in the presence of my
>   heavenly Father;
33 but whoever denies me in the presence of others,
>   will be denied by me in the presence of my heavenly
>   Father.

34 Do not suppose that I came to bring peace to the earth.
>   35 I came with a sword to divide:
>   a man against his father,
>   a daughter against her mother,
>   a daughter-in-law against her mother-in-law.
36 A person's enemies will be members of one's own family.

37 Whoever loves father or mother more than me
>   is not worthy of me;
whoever loves son or daughter more than me
>   is not worthy of me;
38 whoever does not take up the cross
>   and follow me is not worthy of me.

39 Those who try to preserve their life will lose it,
>   and those who lose their life for my sake will find it.

---

7. "Hell" is literally "Gehenna," a Greek term for a place of fiery destruction.

40 Whoever accepts you accepts me;
>   whoever accepts me accepts the one who sent me.
41 Whoever accepts the claims of a true prophet
will receive a prophet's reward;
42 whoever accepts the claims of a truly righteous person
will receive the reward of the righteous;
whoever gives a cup of cold water to one of these little ones
because he is a disciple will not lose his reward.

You can count on what I've said.

This passage is poetic because of the balanced structure throughout, which is infused with antithetical concepts (veiled/revealed, dark/light, whisper/broadcast, body/soul, confession/denial) that elevate the text from prose to poetry. The idea of dividing family members could be drawn from Micah 7:6.

Jesus' Message for John the Baptist (11:3–19)

3 Take a message to John, who asks if I am the One
or is there another messiah yet to come?
4 Tell him what you hear and see:
5 *the blind receive their sight,*
the lame walk, the lepers cleansed,
the deaf hear, the dead are raised,
and the poor are given God's message.[8]

6 If you aren't tripped up by what you think of me,
you are blessed.

---

8. The statements in italics come from various verses in Isaiah (26:19; 29:18; 35:5; 42:18; 61:1).

7 Jesus began to speak to the crowds about John:

What scene attracted you into the wilderness?
A reed swayed by every wind?
8 What did you go out to see?
Someone dressed in fine robes?
Those who wear fine clothes luxuriate in king's palaces.
9 What did you go out to see? A prophet?
Yes, I tell you, and one greater than a prophet.
10 This is the one about whom it is written,
I am sending my messenger ahead of you,
who will prepare your way before you.[9]

11 Of all those born of women no one has risen
   to be greater than John the Baptist.
Yet the least in the kingdom is greater than he.

12 From the days of John the Baptist until now
   the kingdom of heaven forcefully advances,
   and violent men attack it.[10]

13 All the prophets foretold the times until John appeared,
   14 who is the Elijah predicted to come.
15 If you have ears to hear, you will accept him.

16 But to what will I compare this generation?
   It is like children sitting in the marketplaces
   calling out to one another,

---

9. Jesus altered Malachi 3:1 by adding "ahead of you" (perhaps influenced by the Greek version of Exod 23:20) to emphasize John as his forerunner, and by changing the pronouns from first person to second person so as to have Yahweh address the Messiah.

10. The Greek can also be interpreted to mean "the kingdom suffers violence because violent people seize it."

> 17 "We played the flute for you, but you did not dance;
> we sang a dirge, but you did not mourn."

18 For John came neither feasting nor drinking,
and they say, "He's demon-possessed."
19 The Son of Man came feasting and drinking,
and they say, "Look, a glutton and a drinker,
a friend of tax collectors and sinners!"

Yet Wisdom is vindicated by her works.[11]

Jesus' message, presented in prophetic style, overflows with a mixture of figures of speech ("reed swaying in the wind"), enigmatic expressions ("the kingdom forcefully advances, and violent men attack it" and "Wisdom is vindicated by her works"), a revised OT citation (Mal 3:1), and folk poetry ("we played the flute for you, but you did not dance/we sange a dirge for you, but you did not mourn").

Jesus' Prayer and Invitation (11:25–30)

25–26 I praise you, Father, Master of heaven and earth,
that it was your good pleasure to veil
these truths from the shrewd and intelligent
and to reveal them to children.

27 No one knows the Son except the Father;
no one knows the Father except the Son
and anyone to whom the Son chooses to reveal him—
these are the ones given to me by my Father.

---

11. The best manuscript support (ℵ B W MSS known by Jerome) favors "works." Inferior support (B² C D L Maj) read "children" as a result of harmonization to Luke 7:35, a parallel verse.

28 Come to me, all you who are heavy and weary,
   and I will relieve you.
29–30 Shoulder my yoke by learning from me—
   my yoke is easy and my load is light,
   my heart is gentle, and I am meek.
I will give your souls repose.[12]

The three stanzas of this poem are connected by the theme of revelation. The Father reveals the truths of Jesus' teachings, not to the intelligent, but to those who are as receptive as children; the Father reveals the Son to those whom the Father has chosen—and to no one else; the Son reveals himself (as gentle and meek) to those weary ones who come to him. These are the ones (chosen by the Father) who drop their heavy yokes and get yoked up with Jesus, who metaphorically presented himself as an oxen looking for fellow oxen. In ancient times oxen were yoked together.

Jesus, the Chosen Servant (12:18–21)

18 Look at my Servant, my chosen One,
   my beloved, my soul's delight.
When I pour my Spirit upon him,
   he will restore the world to justice—
19 not by raising his voice or crying out,
   so as to be heard in the streets.
20 He will not snap a bruised, bent reed;
   he will not snuff a smoldering wick,
for he has come to restore the way of justice
   21 and give all nations reason for hope.

---

12. Isaiah 28:12; Jeremiah 6:16

This quotation essentially comes from the Hebrew version of Isaiah 42:1–4, with some alterations—especially the words "my chosen One," as well as the last line, which follows the Greek version (lit. "the Gentiles will hope in his Name"). The dual imagery in v. 20 of not snapping a bruised reed and not snuffing out a smoldering wick is a powerful way of saying that the Messiah does not destroy those who are broken or faltering.

The Reason for Parables (13:11–17)

11 You are given understanding
of the mysteries of the kingdom of God,
> but they are not.

12 To those who have, more will be given,
and they will enjoy abundance;
> but those who have nothing will lose even that.

13 This is why I speak to them in parables, so that:
> looking, they do not see,
> listening, they do not hear.

14 With them is fulfilled the prophecy of Isaiah:

Though they hear with their ears,
> *they do not comprehend;*
though they see with their eyes,
> *they do not understand.*

15 *These people have impenetrable hearts.*
> *Their ears are so shut*
> *and their eyes so closed,*
they cannot receive illumination
> *or comprehend the truth.*

If they grasped anything,
  they would turn their hearts to me
and I would heal them completely.

16 But your eyes are blessed, for they see,
  and your ears, for they hear.
17 I assure you, many prophets and righteous people
desired to see what you see, but did not see it,
  and to hear what you hear, but did not hear it.

This poem is built around a quotation that comes from the Greek version of Isaiah 6:9–10. This is the most often cited OT passage in the NT; it appears here, Mark 4:12; Luke 8:10; John 12:40; Acts 28:26–27; Romans 8:11. It is also quoted in P. Oxyrhynchus 406, an early Christian document (c. 200) in which the writer is appealing to this Scripture to explain why certain people [the Jews?] did not realize that Jesus was the Christ. (See Comfort and Dreisbach, *The Many Gospels of Jesus*, 265–266, for more on this text.) Paul took the same approach in Acts 28:26–27. Indeed, this passage is an apt description of why the religious establishment of Jesus' day rejected him as the Messiah. The rest of the poem expands the same theme as the citation by using terms of sight and hearing (each of which appears five times in the poem) to show that only with open hearts and receptive spirits can people really see and hear God's truths.

Yearnings for Jerusalem (23:37–39)

37 O Jerusalem, O Jerusalem,
even though you murdered the prophets
and stoned the messengers God sent you,

> I have so often desired to gather you together
> as a hen gathers her chicks under her wings.
>> But you refused to let me.
> 38 So now your temple will be left to you, abandoned[13]—
> 39 and you won't see me again until you cry,
> *"Blessed is the one who comes to us*
> *in the name of the Lord!"*[14]

This is an extraordinary poem because it shows Jesus presenting himself as a mother hen longing to gather her children together. This is is one of those rare instances in which Jesus uses a feminine image for himself. Then, the poem quickly shifts to the image of Jesus, as God, abandoning his temple because he has been abandoned by his people in Jerusalem. They would not see him again until they wanted him to come and called on his name.

Jesus Foretells the Future (24:4–36)

> 4 Beware that no one deceives you.
> 5 For many will claim to be me—
> when they declare, 'I am the Christ,'
> they will lead many astray.
>
> 6 Don't be disturbed when you hear of wars
>> and reports about wars,
> because these must happen before this world ends.
> 7 Nation will war against nation,
>> and kingdom against kingdom,
> with famines and earthquakes here and there.

---

13. This word (*eremos*) is found in many of the best manuscripts (P77 ℵ C D W); it is absent in B L.

14. Psalm 118:26.

8 All these signal the onset of birth pains.

9 Hated by everyone because of your allegiance to me,
>   you will be arrested, tortured, and killed.
10 Many will fall prey to unbelief,
>   hating and betraying others who have faith.
11 Many false prophets will come
>   and lead many astray.
12 Because rebellion will intensify,
>   the love of many will grow cold as ice.
13 But those who endure to the very end will be rescued.
14 And this good message of the kingdom
>   will be proclaimed throughout the world,
as a testimony to all the nations;
and then the end will come.

15 So when you see the sacrilegious object
placed in the sacred place, the desecration will begin,
as was spoken of by the prophet Daniel[15]
>   (let the reader understand).
16 Then those in Judea must escape to the mountains;
17 the one on the housetop must not go down
>   to take what is in the house;
18 the one in the field must not turn back to get a coat.
19 What misery awaits those who are pregnant
and those who are nursing in those days!
20 Pray your escape won't be in winter or on a sabbath.
21 For at that time there will be great anguish,
>   such as has not ever been—
>   from the beginning of the world until now,
>   no, and never will be!

---

15. Daniel 9:27; 11:31; 12:11.

22 And if those days had not been shortened,
    no one would be rescued;
but for the sake of God's chosen people
    those days will be cut short.

23 Then if anyone says to you,
'Look! Here is the Christ' or 'There he is!'
    do not believe it.
24 For false christs and false prophets will appear
    and produce great signs and omens,
to lead astray, if possible, even the chosen ones.
25 Take note, I have told you beforehand.
26 So, if they say to you, 'Look! He is in the wilderness,'
    do not go out.
If they say, 'Look! He is in some secret chamber,'
    do not believe it.

27 For as the lightning flashes in the east
    and is manifest as far as the west,
so will be the Parousia of the Son of Man.
28 Wherever the corpse is,
    the vultures gather together.

29 Immediately after the anguish of those days,
    the sun will be blotted out,
        the moon will not beam;
    stars will fall from the sky,
        and celestial powers will quiver.[16]

30 Then the sign of the Son of Man
    will appear in heaven.

---

16. Isaiah 13:10; 34:4.

All the peoples of the earth will be in anguish
> when they see the Son of Man on the clouds of heaven
> coming with magnificent power and glory.

31 With loud trumpet call, he will send out his angels
> from one end of heaven to the other

to gather together his chosen ones
> from the four corners of the earth.

32 The fig tree provides an illustration
> you must learn:

as soon as its branches show tender buds
> and sprout leaves,

you know that summer is near.

33 So also, when you see all these things,
> you know that he is near—
>> just outside the door.

34 Believe me, this nation will not pass away
> until all these things have taken place.

35 Heaven and earth will pass away,
> but my words will not pass away.

36 But about that day and hour no one knows,
> neither the angels of heaven, nor the Son,
> but only the Father.

This poem is a prophetic proclamation of destruction and doom modeled after OT prophecies found in chapters like Jeremiah 6 and Ezekiel 30.

2

The Gospel according to Mark

Prologue Poem to the Gospel of Jesus Christ (1:1–3)

1 The Gospel of Jesus Christ, God's Son,[1]
2 began as Isaiah the prophet had written:

See what I am doing:
I am sending my messenger ahead of you
    to prepare the way before you.

Before the people see your face,
3 they will hear the messenger's voice
shouting in the wilderness,
    "Make a way for the Lord.
    Clear the paths for his coming."

Mark's Gospel begins in poetic fashion with the fusion of two OT citations. The first one comes from Malachi 3:1 (and perhaps Exod 23:20); the second comes from the Greek version of Isaiah 40:3. The image is that of a forerunner or herald preparing the way for a royal person's coming by verbal proclamation. This was a common event in antiquity.

---

1. Though some manuscripts (ℵ* Θ) do not include "God's Son," the expression has good documentary attestation (ℵ² A B D L W).

Severe Discipleship (9:42–50)

42 If any of you causes a young believer to fall into sin,
you would be better off if a heavy millstone
> were hung around your neck
> and you were thrown into the sea.

43 If your hand causes you to commit sin, cut it off;
it is better for you to enter eternal life maimed
> than to have two hands
> as you're thrown into hell's[2] undying fire.[3]

45 If your foot causes you to trip into sin, cut it off;
it is better for you to enter eternal life lame
> than to have two feet
> as you fall into hell.

47 If your eye causes you to fall into sin, tear it out;
it is better for you to enter God's kingdom
> with one eye than to have two eyes
> as you're thrown into hell,
>> 48 where the maggot is never satisfied,
>> the flames never die,
>> 49 and everyone is salted with fire.

50 Salt is good only if it doesn't lose its zest,
which cannot be recovered once it's lost.
Be salty, and be at peace with one another.

This passage is poetic by virtue of the symmetry exhibited in the stanzas, as well as by Jesus' use of hyperbole in what he says should be done to anyone or anything that causes of-

---

2. "Hell" in Greek is "Gehenna," a place of fiery destruction.

3. The best manuscripts (ℵ B C L W 0274) do not include verses 44 and 46, which have the same wording as in v. 48. Some scribe added these verses, which appears in other manuscripts (A D Maj), as a kind of poetic refrain.

fense. The poem ends with the image of salt. The expression "salted with fire" is best explained by the Jewish practice of salting a sacrifice. The meal offering was roasted first and then sprinkled with salt to symbolize the perfection of the offering (Lev 2:13). Since salt made the grain good to eat, this act indicated, in a figurative way, that the sacrifice was acceptable to God. Jesus may have had this ritual in mind when he said that every one of his followers would have to be "salted with fire" in order to be made acceptable before God.

3

The Gospel according to Luke

The Annunciation to Zechariah (1:11–17)

11–12 An angel appeared to Zechariah and said,

    13 Don't fear, Zechariah.
Your prayers and Elizabeth's were heard by God.
Your wife will give birth to a son,
    and you will call him John.
14 Many will rejoice when he is born,
and he will be your pride and joy.
    15 In the Lord's eyes he will be magnificent,
for he will be filled with the sacred Spirit
    while in his mother's womb.
    He will never partake of wine or alcohol.[1]
    16 He will turn many of Israel's people
    to the Lord their God,
17 as he goes before him
in the spirit and power of Elijah[2]
    to turn the fathers' hearts to their children
    and the disobedient to righteous people,
as he makes the people ready to receive the Lord.

---

1. See Leviticus 10:9; Numbers 6:3, which speak of prohibitions for those who take the Naazarie vow, one of which is to abstain from drinking any alcohol.

2. See Malachi 3:1; Matthew 11:14.

Luke 1:13–17 is set as a poem in *Novum Testamentum Graece* (27th edition). This poem celebrates the birth of John who would become the Lord's forerunner.

The Annunciation, the angel Gabriel's poem (1:30–33, 35)

> 30 There's no need to fear, Mary.
> God favors you so much
> > 31 you will conceive and birth a son,
> > whom you will name Jesus.
>
> 32 To this magnificent one, called the Most High's Son,
> the Lord God will give David's throne.
> 33 He will reign over Israel[3] forever
> > in a kingdom that never ends.
> 35 God's sacred Spirit will envelope you
> and the Most High will cover[4] you
> > with his potent presence
> so that the one being conceived
> > will be called God's sacred Son.

No matter what the source of this passage (Luke may have heard it from Mary when he did his historical research—see Luke 1:1–4), Luke is responsible for the final wording of this poem in Greek. By comparing it with the parallel wording in Matthew 1:20–21 (which is curt), one sees that Luke embellished the depiction of how the Most High through his divine Spirit would enact the mysterious conception. In the Greek of the last stanza, Luke uses three verbs (*epeluesetai* = "will envelope"; *episkiasei* = "will cover"; *klethesetai* = "will be called") to beautifully culminate the poem.

3. Literally, "Jacob."
4. Or, "overshadow."

The Magnificat, Mary's poem (1:46-55)

46 Lord, I extol you with all my soul.
47 O God my Savior, joy leaps in my spirit
48 for your compassion on me, your humble servant.
Generations will know I was blessed by you.
49 O mighty God, you have been so good to me—
Praise your sacred Name!

50 While your mercy flows to all who revere you,
>even generation after generation,
51 your hands are strong against the proud,
>whose haughtiness you scatter as sand.

52 You topple potentates from their thrones,
>and lift up the lowly in your arms.
53 You feed the hungry until they're full
>and consign the rich to emptiness.

54-55 You have not forgotten your promises to our fathers,
>to Abraham, and his everlasting offspring.
O Lord, you have come to rescue Israel!

No matter what the source of this passage (Luke probably heard it from Mary when Luke did his historical research—see Luke 1:1-4), Luke is responsible for the final wording of this poem in Greek. Though this passage is usually called a song, there is no evidence that it was actually sung. In any event, its wording is like a psalm of praise—in many ways reflecting Hannah's psalm of praise recorded in 1 Samuel 2:1-10. The term "magnificat" (which means "glories") comes from the first word in the Latin Vulgate of Luke 1:46. The first word in Greek is *megalunei*, which I have rendered as "extol."

The Benedictus, Zechariah's poem (1:67–79)

67 John's father, Zechariah, overflowing
with the Holy Spirit prophesied:

68 Praise the Lord God of Israel
    who has now visited his people
    and come to set us free
69 by raising up from David's dynasty
a deliverer with power as strong as a ram's horn.
70 What was spoken through his holy prophets of old
has now been realized—
    71 that we would be rescued
    from the grip of all who hate us.
72 The mercy promised to our fathers
    has now been shown to us,
73 for God has not forgotten the promises
of his sacred covenant—
the oath he swore to Abraham, our father,
    74 that we would freed from our enemies
to serve our God in his presence,
    75 with fearlessness, purity, and righteousness
    throughout all our living days on earth.
76 You, my child, will be called prophet of the Most High,
his forerunner preparing roads before him,
    77 making it known that salvation is coming
    to the people needing their sins forgiven.
78 By God's tender mercies, heaven's sun
will visit us when the eastern dawn springs,[5]

---

5. Literally, "the *Anatole* [the eastern sun] will visit us from heaven." The verb "will visit" is future tense in the Greek (*episkepsetai*) according to the best manuscript evidence (P4 א B L W). It is past tense in א² A C D, a change scribes made in comformity to Luke 1:78 (the second line of the first poetic stanza). Even though the verb is future, the expression in

> 79 luminating those who sit under the shadow of death,
> lighting a path for them to walk in peace.

No matter what the source of this passage (Luke may have heard it from Zechariah when Luke did his historical research—see Luke 1:1–4), Luke is responsible for the final wording of this poem in Greek. Though this passage is usually called a song, it is actually a poetic prophecy. It is called the "Benedictus" (meaning "praise be") because this is the first word in the Latin Vulgate.

The Nunc Dimitis, Simeon's poem (2:28–32)

> 28 Simeon took Jesus' in his arms and praised God:
>
> 29 Sovereign Master, let your servant
> have quietus, even as you promised.
> 30 I have seen the Savior with my very own eyes
> 31 whom you have given for everyone's salvation.
> 32 He is light; he is revelation—for all the nations!
> He is the glory of your people, Israel!

This poem probably came to Luke through oral tradition because Simeon would not have been alive at the time Luke composed his gospel. In any event, Luke was responsible for writing the poem in Greek. This beautifully compacted poem is filled with visual images: eyes, light, revelation,

---

context points to Christ's first advent—his visitation as the sunrising or dayspring from the heavens to the earth. The word *Anatole* has a secondary meaning: branch or shoot (see BAGD, 62), which was used in the OT Greek version to translate the Hebrew word for "Branch" (Isa 11:1; Jer 23:5; 33:15; Zech 3:8; 6:12). The dual image celebrates Christ's coming as the dayspring and Branch. In fact, this is the only NT reference to the OT messianic title, "Branch." I attempted to catch the dual idea of the dawning light and the branch with the expression "the eastern dawn springs."

and glory. Simeon magnified his seeing of God's light (in Jesus) as being prophetic of the enlightenment yet to dawn on all humanity, both Gentiles and Jews. The title of the poem "Nunc Dimitis" comes from the first two words in the Latin Vulgate, which mean "now dismiss [your servant]." In English I have used the words "let [your servant] have quietus."

The Voice in the Wilderness (3:4–6)

4 It is written in the book of the prophet Isaiah:
  A voice crying in the wilderness:

  "Prepare the road for the Lord's coming.
    Straighten out the paths.
    5 Fill in every valley.
    Level every mountain and hill.

  Then the crooked will be straightened,
    and the rough paths made smooth
    6 so that all humanity can see him coming—
    bringing salvation from God!"

This poetic citation about John the Baptist comes from the Greek version of Isaiah 40:3–5. However, Luke's version does not include the line in Isaiah 40:5 about the glory of the Lord being seen, which precedes the line about all humanity seeing the salvation of God.

Jesus, the Anointed One (4:17–19)[6]

17 He took the book of the prophet Isaiah,
unrolled the scroll, and located the passage
which he then read aloud:

> 18 *The Lord's Spirit is with me*
> *because he has anointed me and sent me*
> *to proclaim good news to the poor*
> *to announce freedom for the captives*
> *to heal the blind*
> *to liberate the oppressed*
> 19 *to announce the year of Lord's acceptance.*

The poem is carried by the five infinitive phrases. Some manuscripts (A Θ Ψ) add another infinitive phrase: "to heal the broken-hearted." But there is strong testimony against it (ℵ B D L W), coupled with the likelihood that scribes added the phrase to make it conform to Isaiah 61:1–2. The last two words "Lord's acceptance" are purposefully ambiguous; they connote the Lord's acceptance of the people's acceptance of him.

The Blessings and Miseries (6:20–26)

> 20 Those of you who suffer poverty are blessed,
>   for you will be rich in God's kingdom.
> 21 Those who experience hunger are blessed,
>   for you will be filled to the full.
> Those who lament their condition are blessed,
>   for you will laugh in celebration.

---

6. The citation comes from the Greek version of Isaiah 61:1–2.

22 Those of you hated, excluded, reviled, and defamed
> because of your stand for the Son of Man are blessed.
That is how their ancestors treated the prophets.
23 But you will jump for joy
> because of your rich reward in heaven.

24 Those of you who are rich now will be miserable,
> for you've already got all you'll ever get.
25 Those who are satiated now will be miserable,
> for you will go hungry.
26 Those who are laughing now will be miserable,
> for you will mourn and weep.

Beware when everyone lauds you,
> for that is the way the false prophets
> were treated by their ancestors.

This poem has the same poetic structure and features as the Beatitudes in Matthew 5:3–12, but Luke's version differs from Matthew's lexically. Furthermore, Luke includes a pronouncement of miseries (traditionally called "woes").

The Eye, the Body's Lamp (11:34–36)

34 The eye is the lamp of the body.
> If your eye has clarity,
your whole body will be illumined;
> but if your eye is bad,
your whole body will be darkened.

35 If the light turns into darkness,
> what gloom that will be!
36 But if your entire being is flooded with light,
> as from a lamp's beaming rays,
you will be fully illumined
> without even a trace of darkness.

The beauty of this poem is in the extended image of the relationship between light, the eye, and one's being (body), as well as the enigmatic twist that interior light can become darkness creating internal gloom (cf. Matt 6:22-23).

Setting Earth on Fire (12:49-53)

49 I came to set the earth on fire!
   How I desire it were already kindled!
50 I will be immersed in flames—
   what stress until it's all over!

51 I did not come to give earth peace and union.
   No, my coming creates division!

52 From now on five in one family will be divided,
   three against two and two against three:
   53 father against son
   and son against father,
   mother against daughter
   and daughter against mother,
   mother-in-law against her daughter-in-law
   and daughter-in-law against mother-in-law.

This poem is one of the few lyrical poems expressed by Jesus in that it pertains to his own personal inner anguish, verbalized in the form of an inner flame he wanted to spread all over earth. (See next poem and note.)

Signs of the Time (Luke 12:54-56)

54 When you see a cloud rising in the west,
   you know a rainstorm is brewing.
55 When you feel the south wind blowing,
   you know scorching heat is coming.

56 If you can discern the changing faces of earth and sky,
   why can't you discern what has come to you now?

In Luke 12:49–56 we see two separate poems, one following the other thematically. The first has a powerful image of Jesus casting a firestorm on earth, one that would create division. (Though it takes some imagination to see how fire divides, it was used in war to keep one's enemy away.) In the Matthew parallel passage (10:34–36), the image is a sword. The second poem continues the theme of the first in that it alludes to the storm created by Jesus' parousia.

Camel through a Needle's Eye (18:24–25)

24 How difficult it is for a rich person
   to enter God's kingdom.
25 It is easier for a camel
   to thread its way through a needle's eye
   than for the rich to squeeze into God's kingdom.

This passage reveals a typical format used by Jesus: a bold statement followed by an aphorism—in this case, it is quite hyperbolic.

Jesus Foretells the Future (21:8–21)

8 Beware that you are not deceived.
For many will claim to be me,
   saying, 'I am the one!' and 'the day has come!'
Do not follow them.

9 Don't be disturbed when you hear
   of wars and revolutions,
for these things must happen first,
   but the end will not immediately follow.

10 Nation will war against nation,
>   and kingdom against kingdom.
11 There will be tremendous earthquakes,
>   and famines and plagues in various places;
and there will be awful portents
>   and great signs in heaven.

12 But before all these things occur,
>   they will persecute you and arrest you.
>   They will hand you over to synagogues and prisons,
and you will be brought before kings and governors
>   because of your allegiance to me.
13 This will be your chance to be my witnesses.
14 But don't prepare your defense in advance;
15 for I will give you the words and wisdom
>   that none of your opponents can refute.

16 You will be betrayed by parents and brothers,
>   by friends and relatives;
and they will put some of you to death.
17 You will be hated by everyone
>   because of your allegiance to me.
18 But not a hair of your head will perish.
19 By your perseverance you will win your souls.

20 When you see Jerusalem surrounded by armies,
>   realize it will soon be destroyed.
21 Those in Judea must flee to the mountains,
>   those in Jerusalem must depart,
>   and those in the country must not enter it.
22 For these days of vengeance
>   will fulfill all that is written.

23 What miseries await those who are pregnant
>   and to those who are nursing infants!

> For there will be great disaster on the earth
> > and anger expressed against this people.
> 24 They will be slaughtered by the sword
> > and taken as captives among all nations.
> Jerusalem will be trampled down by the Gentiles,
> > until the period of the Gentiles is complete.
>
> 25 There will be signs in the sun, moon, and stars.
> The nations on earth will be distressed
> > and overwhelmed by the roaring of the sea's surf.
> 26 People will be terrified
> > by what is coming upon the world
> as the powers of the heavens are shaken down.
> 27 Then they will see the Son of Man coming in a cloud
> > with magnificent power and glory.
>
> 28 Now when these things begin to take place,
> > stand and look up,
> because your redemption is near.

This poem is a prophetic proclamation of destruction and doom modeled after OT prophecies found in chapters like Jeremiah 6 and Ezekiel 30.

Jesus' Prohibition against Weeping (23:28–31)

> 28 Daughters of Jerusalem, do not weep for me.
> Weep for yourselves and your children.
> 29 The days are coming when they will say,
> > "Blessings on barren women—
> > the wombs that do not give birth
> > and the breasts that never nursed."
> 30 They will begin to say to the mountains,
> > "fall on us," and to the hills, "bury us."

> 31 For if they do these things to me
>   while the tree is watered and green,
>   what will they do when it is dry?

This poem has a rich mixture of imagery, beginning with an ironic "blessing" for women who don't bring children in a tumultuous world, and ending with an agricultural metaphor of impending drought (after the Lord, the living tree, leaves this world).

4

The Gospel according to John

Prologue Poem to Christ, the God-Word (1:1–18)

1 As to a beginning, the Word has always lived
 near the face of God's presence.
2 The Word who is himself divine
 has always been God's essence.

3 Creation flowed through him
and nothing can exist without being in him—
 all is alive with his vibrant life;
 4 every being has life and light from him.
5 The light keeps shining in the darkness,
 which has never grasped it.

6 God sent a man named John
to foretell the coming of the Light
 so people would welcome him with faith.
7 He was God's herald sent to signal
the epiphany of him who would come
 to enlighten everyone.
8 John was not the light,
 just a witness to its coming presence.
9–10 When the true Light came to the world he made,
 they did not recognize their Maker.
11 When he came to his very own people,
 they did not receive him either.

12 Yet everyone who welcomed him—
> by trusting what he claimed—
was given the privilege of becoming God's child,
> 13 not of human seed, plan, or passion,
but of God's regeneration.

14 The Word, becoming human, became
> God's sacred tabernacle dwelling among us—
> we saw his splendor and glory;
> the honor a Father gives his only Son
glowed from him in unique effulgence
overflowing with truth and lovingkindness.

15 (This was the One John the Baptist extolled:
"he who came after I did ranks far ahead of me,
> for he has always been.")
16 Yes, of his fullness have all we received—
grace flowing from grace, grace in abundance,
> a replenishing fount of lovingkindness.

17 So different is this than the law
> which was given us by Moses.
Grace and truth came to us
> in the very person of Christ Jesus.

18 Never before had anyone seen God,
but the One and Only, who is himself God[1]
> and nearest to the Father's heart,
has been explaining him to us.

In my opinion, the prologue to John's Gospel is the most profound poem in the New Testament. I have pondered this

---

1. "The One and Only, who is himself God" is a translation of *monogenes theos*, which is supported by the earliest and best manuscripts (P66 P75 ℵ B). Later manuscripts read *monogenes huios* (one and only Son).

poem and mediatated on it for nearly 40 years, and I am still intrigued by its illumination, as well as awed by its elusiveness. The first stanza is alluringly insightful. It speaks of the Logos (the Word) as being with God and being God from an indeterminate beginning. Its profound brevity inspires questions and reverence. The second stanza speaks of the Word's participation in creation, both in its genesis and sustenance. All that is alive is alive with his life; this life-force inherent in creation has been the divine light to humanity (see Rom 1:18)—even before the Word became incarnate in the person of Jesus. But there is also a second level of meaning here: Christ's life became the light of men (John 8:12). Double meaning continues in the next lines, which says the darkness *ou katelaben*, meaning (1) the darkness did not grasp (understand) the light, and (2) the darkness did not overpower (conquer) the light.

The next three stanzas continue the theme of the light coming to a world of darkness (unbelief and ignorance). John the Baptist was a lamp pointing the way to the bright light. Unfortunately, most rejected this light, but those who accepted it became children of God. The final four stanzas speak of the Word's incarnation so as to be the revelation of God's fullness to those who trusted in him. The writer John used the image of God's glory inhabiting the tabernacle as a backdrop to Jesus being the embodiment of God's grace-giving glory. The final stanza mirrors the first in that (1) both speak of the Word as being God; (2) both indicate the intimate relationship between the Father and Son ("face to face" and "nearest to the Father's heart"); and (3) both tell us that the Son is God's expression/explanation ("the Word" and "he has been explaining him to us"). Thus, the final stanza gives us insight to interpreting the opening of the prologue poem.

The New Birth (3:3, 5–8, 12–15)

> 3 Those who see God's realm and enter it
>   cannot do so with human sight;
> 5 the entrance is found when one is born
>   of the Spirit's living flow.[2]
> 6 While flesh generates only flesh;
>   Spirit generates spirit.[3]
> 7–8 The wind blows wherever it chooses;
>   you can't see where the wind is going
>   or where its breath comes from,
>   even though you hear its sound.
> Those born of Spirit are wind.
>
> 12 If you can't believe these earthly images,
>   how could you ever comprehend heaven,
>   where you have never been?
> 13 The Son of Man[4] is the only one who can ascend into heaven
>   because that is where he came from.
> 14 He will be lifted up like a snake on a stake
> 15 so that everyone who sees him and trusts him
>   will have eternal life instead of death.

---

2. Literally, "water and spirit," which I understand as a hendiadys for the flowing, regenerative power of the Spirit.

3. Literally, "the thing having been born of the Spirit is spirit." I take this to mean that the divine Spirit quickens a person's human spirit, but it could also mean that Spirit generates its own kind—spirit (just as flesh generates its own kind—flesh).

4. Some manuscripts (A Θ Ψ Maj) add "who is in heaven." But better testimony (P66 P75 ℵ B L W) supports the text.

The poem in the original Greek is interrupted by queries from Nicodemus—hence, verses 4, 9–11 are not included. The poetic quality of this passage is found in the use of the Greek word *pneuma* (and the verbal form *pnei*) to connote several ideas in one: wind, breath, human spirit, and the divine Spirit. The person's spirit who is quickened by God's Spirit takes on the quality of being like the wind—thus, "those born of the spirit are wind." These regenerated ones can enter God's realm. Another aspect of the poem is found in Jesus' allusion to the snake that Moses lifted up on a stake, which gave life to all who looked at it (Num 21:9). He used this as a metaphor for his crucifixion: those who see the crucified one and trust him for their salvation will receive eternal life.

Tribute to the Only Son (3:16–21)

16 God was moved by love to send his only Son
 for the world's salvation.
Everyone who trusts the Son will be rescued
 from destruction and be given life eternal.

17 God did not send the Son into the world
 to condemn it but to rescue it.
18 Those who trust him are not condemned;
 but those who don't are condemned already,
because they have not believed
 in the proclamation of God's only Son.

19 When the Light came into the world,
 people loved their darkness rather than light.
20 They hid from the light because they practiced evil
 and feared their deeds would be exposed.

21 Truth-seekers welcome the light
    where they see how to live in God.

Many commentators (including myself) think Jesus finished his speech to Nicodemus in 3:15 and that John the writer began his own discourse in 3:16 (finishing in 3:21). The future orientation of this passage (i.e., it addresses people who lived during and after the time of Christ) seems to affirm this (Comfort and Hawley, *Opening John's Gospel and Epistles*, 52–53). This poetic passage displays John's favorite dichotomous images: belief versus unbelief, eternal life versus destruction, light versus darkness, salvation versus condemnation.

John the Baptist Extols Jesus, the Bridegroom (3:27–36)

27 No one can do anything
except what's granted from heaven.
28 You have heard me say, "I am not the Christ.
I was sent to prepare the way before him."

29 It is the bridegroom who embraces the bride!
The bridegroom's friend is privileged to stand near him—
just to hear him fills my heart with incredible joy!

30 While I diminish, he will be magnified.

31 The earthly one is earthbound—
beyond this sphere his language cannot expand.
The heavenly One, superior to everyone,[5]
32 has told us what he's seen and heard,
yet no one accepts his testimony.

---

5. Some manuscripts (P36 P66 B L W) include the phrase "superior to everyone" (lit. "is over all") twice—both at the beginning and the end of the verse; other manuscripts (P75 ℵ D) just once.

> 33 But whoever has accepted his testimony as true
> has placed his seal of approval on God's Son
> 34 as the one who speaks the truth
> and pours out the immeasurable Spirit.
>
> 35 Because the Father loves the Son,
> he has placed everything in his hands.
> 36 Whoever trusts the Son is given eternal life;
> whoever doesn't, will not see the next life
> and cannot escape God's anger.

John the Baptist used two primary poetic images in this passage in comparing himself to Jesus, who is superior. First, he pictures Jesus as the bridegroom who has the bride (an image for God's people), while he is but the bridegroom's friend. Second, he pictures Jesus as the heavenly One who speaks heavenly language, while he himself is an earthbound human who speaks earthly language.

Worship in Spirit (4:23–24)

> 23 The age is coming—and now is here—
> when the genuine worshipers
> will not worship the Father
> here on this mountain or even in Jerusalem.
> The age is coming—and now is here—
> when the genuine worshipers
> will worship the Father in spirit and truth.
> 24 Since God is Spirit,
> those who worship him must do so in spirit—
> these are the ones the Father seeks.

A more free rendering of this poem is as follows:

Many worshipers seek temples and mountain peeks
but they're immured inside the traditions they make,
unable to receive Spirit God whose presence exceeds
not only earth, sky, and sea, but everything man creates.
Because God is Spirit those who really worship God must do
 so in spirit—
these are the ones the Father seeks to be his priests.

Feast of the Laborers (4:32, 34–37)

32 I eat food you haven't seen,
> 34 for I am satiated with doing the will
> of the One who sent me.

35 You have a saying, "harvest won't come
> for another four months."

But I say, "lift your eyes and peer
> at the bright grains waving in the wind.

Go reap your wages by gathering
> wheat into the barns of everlasting life,

36 where sowers and reapers feast together,
> enjoying each other's labor.

37 This gives full meaning to another saying,
> "one sows and another reaps."

This poem is sustanined by agricultural imagery, in which Jesus incorporates two agricultural "sayings" popular in his day.

The Son's Union with the Father (5:19–30)

19 Here is the truth about the Son:
> he can do nothing by himself,

for he relies on his Father for everything,
> doing what the Father reveals to him,
> living and working in union with him.

20 Because the Father loves his Son
    he unveils himself to him in every way—
with more revelations yet to come,
    miraculous signs that will astonish you.

21 As the Father quickens the dead
and raises them to life, so the Son
can enliven anyone he chooses.

22 The Father has withheld his judgment,
entrusting the judgment of people to his Son,
23 so all may honor him as they do the Father.
Whoever refuses to honor the Son
refuses the Father who sent him.

24 Here is truth to those who accept my message
    and put their trust in him who sent me:
you have escaped the judgment
and migrated from death to life!

25 Here is more truth, just as good:
    the crucial hour is coming—
    no, I should say, is already here—
when the voice of God's Son will shout
to the dead, and all who hear will live!

26 As the Father is life, so is the Son,
    27 who also will judge every person
    because he is the Son of Man.

28 Do not be amazed:
the crucial moment is coming when everyone
in the graves will hear the Son of God's voice;
    29 those who did good will rise to enjoy life,
    those who did evil will rise to face judgment.

30 Because I rely on my Father and do his will,
>   I judge only as I'm told;
>   therefore, my judgment is good.

This is the most extensive poem about the relationship between the Father and the Son in the NT. The poetic aspect is inherent in the depth of abstractions which cause the reader to pause and think of several layers of meaning, as in the image of those who are spiritually dead being quickened by the Son's living voice, as well as all the physically dead.

Jesus' Witnesses (5:31–47)

31 I would never testify about myself,
>   for self-witness cannot establish truth.

32 I have the greatest witness who speaks for me;
>   I know his testimony is true.

33 You sent your messengers to John,
>   34–35 a burning and shining lamp,
>   a luminary you enjoyed for a season.

Why did you refuse his enlightened words
>   when he testified of me, the light?

36 My witness is better than John's:
>   the miracles inspired by my Father—
>   these testify that he was my Sender.

37 Even more, he himself is my witness—
>   the One whose voice you haven't heard,
>   whose visage you haven't discerned.

38 His message is not heartfelt by you
>   because you refuse to trust the one he sent.

39 You believe your search of sacred writings
   is the sure path to life everlasting.
These sacred texts testify of me,
   40 yet you refuse to come to me
   and find everlasting life.

41 Since I do not seek your praise,
   42 I can tell you honestly,
you have no love for God
43 because you refuse to accept the truth
that I have come in my Father's stead.

44 How can you, who seek each others' glory, ever believe?
You don't look for the honor
and praise that comes from the One and Only.[6]

45 Don't think I will accuse you to the Father.
   Moses will!—the one in whom you've trusted.
46 If you believed him, you would believe me too
   since he wrote of me in the sacred texts you hold true.
47 But if you don't believe his writings,
   how will you ever believe my message?

This poem is built on the extended image of a court room scene wherein Jesus brings in five witnesses to validate his claim to deity: the Father, John the Baptist, Jesus' miracles, the OT prophetic Scriptures, and Moses.

---

6. The term "the One and Only" is *tou monou* in Greek, supported by early manuscripts (P66 P75 B W). Other manuscripts (P63 ℵ A D L 33) read *tou monou theou* (the one and only God).

Jesus, the Bread of Life (6:32-33, 35-40, 45-51, 53-58, 63)

32 Manna from heaven? Is that what you crave?
No more working. No more making bread.
I'm not another Moses who came to keep you fed.

33 God has given someone greater than Moses,
    better than manna.
35-40 I'm life's bread come down from heaven.
If you believed in who I am
    you would come to me and eat eternal food.

For I am not only good, I am God's only Son,
    who gives life for death, spirit for flesh,
    heaven for earth, and drink for thirst.

45-51 Come to me and drink. Come to me and eat.
For if you do not eat the flesh of the Son of Man
    you cannot possess eternal life within.
You will die the death of all flesh
    even as your ancestors in the wilderness
    who dropped dead with manna in their mouths.

53-58 My food, my broken flesh, is blood for you to drink.
My food, my outpoured spirit, is resurrection life.
Those who partake will live in me and I them
    even as the Father and I live as one.

63 Drink my words, for they are life-giving spirit.
Eat my truth, for I am living manna.

I did not translate the entire passage of John 6:32–63 because there is so much repetition and because Jesus' speech was often interrupted by comments from his audience. Furthermore, I condensed some longer statements into pithier sayings. In any event, the image of Jesus as the bread of life takes on several transformations in this passage: (1) as the antitype to the manna coming down from heaven to feed the children of Israel, (2) as the bread of God that gives perpetual eternal life, and (3) as the animal sacrifice whose blood and flesh is bread for those who believe Jesus died in order to give them life.

Jesus, the True Shepherd (10:1–5, 7–18, 27–30)

1 Thieves and robbers don't enter the sheepfold
    through the gate; they climb in another way.
2 The shepherd enters through the gate;
    the gatekeeper opens the gate only for him.

3 Each of his sheep hear him calling them
    by name to come out of the fold.
4 When all of his own have come out,
    he leads the way before his sheep.

They follow him because they know his voice.
    They will never follow a stranger—
5 in truth, they will run from him
    because his voice is not familiar.

7–10 Many came before I did,
    claiming to be the shepherd,
but they were thieves and bandits
    who stole, killed, and damaged.

The true sheep did not heed their voices or follow them.
I am their true shepherd and their way to life.

The true sheep, knowing me, hear my voice,
    and leave the sheepfold through me, their gate,
    finding that verdant pastures await.

11 I have come to give them living abundance,
    and for this I will sacrifice my soul.
12 How unlike the hired hands I am,
    who flee for their lives when the wolves come.
13 They're only in it for the money
    and do not care about the sheep's welfare.

14–15 I will lay down my life for them
    because they are my very own—
they know me and I know them,
    just as my Father and I know each other.

16 I have other sheep to gather from another fold.
    Hearing my voice, they will follow me
    into the new flock I am gathering.

17 The Father loves me because I lay my life down
    and I will take it back up again—
18 he has given me this awesome power
    to surrender my soul and then raise it from death.

27 I recognize my true sheep, and they me,
    for they know my voice and follow.
28 Because I have given them everlasting life,
    they can't be snatched from my hands.
29 My Father who has given them to me
    is mightier than any power that would try
    to steal our sheep from his hands.
30 You must know that I and the Father are one!

In John 10:6 the apostle John says Jesus had spoken what is called in Greek *paroimia*, which means "a similitude, a figure of speech, a mysterious saying in which lofty ideas are concealed" (see BAGD, 629; Liddell & Scott, 1342). John 10:1–5 is similar to an allegory or parable but is not completely so in either category. Unlike an allegory, there is no consistent one-to-one correspondence in this passage (e.g., Jesus is both the gate and the shepherd), and it cannot be reduced to one particular truth being taught, as in a parable. As such, John 10:1–5 is a distinct form of literature in the NT (Schnackenburg, *The Gospel of John* 2.284–285) and should be considered more in the category of poetry than narrative. John 10:7–18, 27–30 presents, in poetic fashion, Jesus' expansive interpretation of the similitude.

Glorification (12:23–26)

23 The time has come for the Son of Man to be glorified.
24 A grain must fall into the soil and die,
    or it will stay just a single kernel;
    only the seed that dies can multiply.

25 Loving one's self brings destruction.
Rejecting one's life in this world
    guarantees life in the next.

26 This is the ground into which you must drop
    if you want to rise honored by God.

The poem is built around the image of seed-planting (= death) and seed-sprouting (= life). The poem shifts from what Jesus must do in order to multiply his life in others, to what disciples must also do.

Jesus' Appeal to Receive the Light (12:44–50)

44–46 I am light shining in this world's darkness.
    If you trust me, I will lead you
    out of this blinding darkness into light
where you will see the One who sent me

>   47 and you will hear my message,
>   which brings not judgment but salvation to humanity.
>   48 But if you reject me and my teachings,
>   these words will speak on the last day
>   49 to your condemnation, for in rejecting me
>   you reject the one who granted me the right
>   50 to give eternal life to all who believe.

John's favorite dichotomous images appear in this poem: light/darkness, reception/rejection, salvation/judgment, eternal life/condemnation.

Poems from Jesus' Last Discourse and Prayer (chpts. 14–17)

Jesus' discourse in chapters 14–16 is poetic by virtue of its sublime revelation presented in the form of similitudes (*paroimiai*), according to Jesus' own words (16:25, see discussion on John 10 above). There is no reader who can grasp what Jesus is saying on the first read. It takes many passes to begin to see that he was telling his disciples that his leaving them (for a little while) was for the purpose of dying and rising so as to prepare the way for them to live in God and for God as Spirit to live in them. This is first presented in the image of dwelling places wherein God and the believers can indwell each other just as the Father and Son indwell each other (chapter 14). (In chapter 14, I omitted verses 8 and 22, which include dialogue between Jesus and the disciples.) The image then turns organic—in a presentation of vine and branches living in one another (chapter 15). In the 16th chapter Jesus uses yet another image to express the brevity of his upcoming anguish (crucifixion) compared to the eternal joy his resurrection would create; the image is that of woman in terrible labor giving birth to a child—yet that birth is so awesome that the pain is no longer remembered. After this Jesus stops speaking in similitudes and then tells the disciples plainly about his departure to the Father (16:25–33). This section is consummated by the loftiest prayer in all the NT (chapter 17).

Mutual Indwelling (14:1–31)

1 Your troubled hearts need to rest in God.
    Trust in him as you would trust in me.
2 There is plenty of room in my Father's house—
    I am going away to prepare a place for you.
3 Soon I will return to welcome you in this home
    so that you may live in God, as I do.

4 You should know that I am the way
    to where you are going. Yes, I am the way
6 to the reality of God's life. You cannot come
    to live in God except by living in me.

7 If you had really known me,
    you would have also known the Father.
Look at me—see him and know him!

9 Those who have seen me have seen the Father,
    for I live in him and he in me.
10 Everything I've done and said, I've done through him
    and he through me, for we indwell each other.

11 The miracles I've done with the Father
    should convince you of this.
12 And you all will be able to do the same,
    if you put your trust in me

13–14 Whatever you ask the Father in my presence—
>   I will do it for you
>   so that the Father may be glorified in the Son.
15 Above all, love me and keep my commands.
>   16 And I will ask the Father to give you
> another partner to be with you forever.
17 He is the Spirit who is real to those who know his presence,
>   but not to those in this world who do not see him,
>   or know him. But you know who is—
> right at this moment he is living among you
>   and soon he will be indwelling you.
18 It is I who will come to you when the Spirit comes.
>   I would never leave you as orphans.

19 In a little while, the world will see me no more.
>   But you will see me, and you will live because I live.

20 On that day of my resurrection you will know
I live in the Father and you in me and I in you.

21 Those who know my commandments and keep them
>   are those who love me.
They will be loved by my Father
>   and I will love them and manifest myself in them.

23 My Father and I in the Spirit will come
>   to those who keep my commands and love me—
we will come to make our home with them,
>   so that they may live in us and we in them.

24 Those who don't love me don't keep my commands
>   or the message I gave you from my Father.

25 I have told you these things while I am still here.

26 Your new partner, the Holy Spirit,
> who is none other than my presence given to you
> by my Father, will teach you things yet to come,
> as well as remind you of what I said before.

27 I will leave my peaceful presence with you,
> which is better than any peace the world can give.

28 So don't be troubled that I am about to leave,
> for I am going to the Father who is greater than I.

29 Continue to believe in what I've told you,
> 30 even when the prince of this world comes—
> but he has no claim on me,
> 31 while I am doing what the Father has willed.

Then the world will realize the love I have for him!

Jesus, the True Vine (15:1–17)

1 I am the Vine; my Father, the vineyard's Master.
> 2 He lops off every unproductive branch
> and prunes every fruitful one
> to yield even more than before.

3 You've already been pruned by my word.

4–5 I am the vine and you are the branches.
Live in me and I will live in you.
The branch cannot produce grapes by itself;
> it must draw its life from the stalk.

As I live in those who live in me,
> they will produce many clusters of fruit.

The branch can't grow without juice from the root.
6 If you don't stay attached to me, you will wither away.
And the Master will gather all the useless branches
> and throw them into a burning pile.

7 If you stay attached to me
> by keeping my words alive in you,
you can ask me anything you desire,
> 8 as long it has to do with producing fruit,
for that is how to glorify the Master.

9 As my Father has loved me, I have loved you.
> To live in me is to live in my love.
10 As I obey my Father, you need to obey me,
> 11 then you will stay in my love
> and will overflow with my joy.

12 This is my command I want you to heed:
> love one another as I have loved you.
13 There is no nobler love than to lay down
> one's life for a friend.

14 You are my friends when you do what I command.
15 From here on in, I will not call you servants,
> but my friends, because I will tell you everything
> the Father has revealed to me—and more.

16 You didn't choose me. I chose you to be
> my living branches producing lasting fruit.
Whatever you ask the Father in my presence
> will be given to you.
17 I give you these instructions
> so that you would love one another.

The World's Hatred of the Disciples (15:18–16:4)

18 The world will hate you because it hated me first.
19 The world, who adores its own, will not cherish you
> because you are not one of them.

20 If they listened to the Master, they would listen to you.

21 But they will persecute you, my servants,
   as they did me—
and thereby reject the One who sent me.

22 Their guilt remains, having no excuse for their sins,
23 for in hating me they hated my Father—even when
   24 they had seen so many miraculous signs.
25 Isn't this what the psalmist had written:
   they hated me for no good reason?[7]

26 You will need the Encourager, the Spirit of truth,
   during your days of persecution.
He will come to you from the Father
   and will testify everything about the Son.
27 You will also speak for me because you have been
   with me from the very beginning.

Chapter 16

1 I have told you all this so you don't give up faith.
2 They will throw you out of synagogues.
They will kill you, thinking they are serving God.
3 But they have never known him or me.
4 I am warning you now so that when persecution comes
you will remember I foretold these events.

The Coming of the Spirit-Encourager (16:5–11, 13–15)

5–6 My words about my departure have saddened you—
   yet none of you asks me where I'm going.
7 It is best for you that I depart, because if I don't go,
   the Spirit-Encourager cannot come.
Once I leave, I will send him to you.

---

7. This citation comes from Psalms 35:19; 69:4.

8–11 And once the Spirit of truth comes,
he will convict the world of sin
>because it refuses to believe in me;
he will announce the way to righteousness
>because I will no longer be seen;
he will proclaim that judgment has been done
>because the world's ruler has been condemned.

13 And when the Spirit of truth comes,
>he will guide you into every spiritual reality.
Not speaking from his own volition,
>he will reveal to you what he hears from me
and unravel the events yet to come.

14 He will glorify me by disclosing to you
>whatever he receives from me.
15 All that the Father has and is belongs to me—
this is the reason I can declare
that the Spirit will take what is mine
>and reveal it to you.

Jesus' Soon Return on the Day of Resurrection (16:19–28)

19 In a little while you won't see me;
>in a little while you will see me again.
20 While you weep and mourn for me,
>the world will be happy.

21 But your grief will suddenly turn to joy,
>as when a woman suffering labor pains
>soon forgets her anguish when her child is born.[8]

22 Your sorrow will turn to joy when I see you again.
You will rejoice with a joy that no one can take from you.

---

8. See Micah 4:6 for the same poetic image.

23 On that day you will not need to ask me anything.
But whatever you ask the Father in my Name,
>   he will give it to you.
24 Up until now you have not asked
>   for anything in my Name.
Ask and you will receive full joy.
25 On that day everything will be plain and clear to you—
>   no more similitudes, as I have been using up till now.
I will reveal the Father to you plainly.
26–28 You will know without a doubt
that I came from the Father into the world
and that I am leaving this world to return to him.
And you will know the Father loves you
because you love me and believe I came from him.

Jesus' Prayer for Unity (17:1–26)

1 Father, the hour has come to glorify your Son,
>   so that he may glorify you in return.
>> 2 You have given him the right to grant eternal life
>>   to every person you have gifted to him.
>> 3 And eternal life is knowing you, the true God,
>>   and the one you sent, Jesus Christ.
>> 4 I glorified you on earth by doing the work
>>   you gave me to complete.
>> 5 Bring me, Father, into that glory we shared
>>   before the world was created.

>> 6–8 I revealed you to these disciples you gave me.
>>   These, who were always yours, kept your word
>> and realized that everything I have comes from you—
>>   even more, they believe I was sent by you.

>> 9 This prayer is not for the world
>>   but for those you've given me, for they are yours.

10 Everything that's mine is yours, and yours is mine—
  in them I have been glorified!
11 Since I am coming to you, my sacred Father,
  I will be leaving them in this world
12 from which they need your protecting hand.
  Keep them in the power of my presence
that they may be unified, even as we are one.

When I was with them, I protected them
  by the power of my presence.
  None of them perished except the son of destruction,
  so as to fulfill what was written.
13 But now that I'm coming to you, I pray
  they may experience my fulfilling joy.

14 They have accepted my message,
  for which they will be hated.
Just as the world rejected me,
they will be despised for what they believe.
15 Though they, as I, no more belong to this world,
I'm not asking that you take them from this world;
rather, I pray that you protect them from the evil one
  and make them sacred by your message of truth.

16–18 Just as you sent me into the world,
  I am sending them into the world—
19 But before I do, I give myself as a sacred sacrifice
  so they can really share my sacred place with you.

20 Father, my prayer extends beyond these, my disciples,
  to all who will believe in me through their message.
21 I pray that they all may be one, just as you and I are,
  and that they all may live in us.
Then the world will believe you sent me.

22 The glory and honor you gave me as your Son
    I have given to them, that they may be one
23 as we are—I in them and you in me in perfect unity.
    Then the world will know you sent me
and loved them even as you loved me.

24 Father, I desire that those whom you have given me
    may also be where I am—that they may see
the glorious splendor you've given me
    because you loved me before the world began.

25 Righteous Father, the world hasn't recognized you,
    but I have known you through and through.
26 These, my disciples, have known that you sent me
    because I revealed your presence to them,
and I will do so again and again so that your love for me
    will also be in them as I indwell them.

5

The Book of Acts

Salvation in the Lord's Name (2:16–21)

16 Peter said, "What you have seen and heard is what God spoke
through the prophet Joel about the last days:
17 *I will pour out my Spirit like rain upon all people.*
Sons and daughers will be revived and prophecy.
    Young men will exult in visions.
Old men will revel in dreams.
18 *In those days when I pour my Spirit on my servants,*
both men and women will prophecy.
Before the glorious days unfold,
19 *I will unveil awesome signs in the heavens*
    and reveal on earth omens
of blood, fire, and clouds of smoke
    20 *as the sun becomes dark*
and the moon bleeds red.
21 *Salvation will come to those*
who call on the name of Lord.[1]

This passage is immediately recognizable as a poem by virtue of its pneumatic and apocalyptic imagery. The outpouring of the Spirt, like life-giving rain, revives prophecy, visions, and

---

1. The citation comes from the Greek version of Joel 2:28–32.

dreams—of what God will reveal before the last day through awful portents, dark sun, and bloodred moon.

Jesus, the Risen One (2:24–28)

24 Though you crucified him, God raised him
and freed him from death's awful anguish.
It was impossible for death to keep him in its grip,
25 for this is just as David said of him:

I foresaw that the Lord's presence
would always be with me—so close to me
that he would keep me next to him,
allowing nothing to disturb me.
26 *No wonder my heart is glad,*
   and my tongue shouts his praise.

My body will rest in a place of hope—
   27 *for you will not abandon my soul to Hades*
or allow your holy one to decay.
   28 *You have shown me the path of life*
that leads to your joyous presence.[2]

This psalm, perfect for predicting the resurrection of Jesus, the son of David, is sustained by the image of the believer not being separated by death from God's living presence. This was David's hope, realized in Christ.

Jesus, the Silent Lamb (8:32–33)

32 The Ethiopian eunuch was reading aloud
the passage of Scripture that says,

---

2. The citation comes from the Greek version of Psalm 16:8–11.

He was a sheep led to slaughter,
a silent lamb before its shearer—
not uttering a sound.
33 He was humiliated
when justice was denied him.
Who can speak of his posterity,
since his life was taken from earth?[3]

The image of a lamb being led to slaughter without uttering a sound is a powerful depiction of the way Jesus faced his trial and persecution.

Gentiles Will Seek the Lord (15:16–18)

16 James told the council that their decision accords with the words of the prophets:

I will return, says the Lord,
to restore David's collapsed tent, to repair its broken seams.
I will restore it from ruins, and build it as it used to be,

17 so that those who were left outside can come inside
to seek my presence—I am speaking of all the Gentiles
whom I have called to be my own.[4]

18 The Lord has spoken, who made this known long ago.[5]

James selected Amos 9:11–12 to characterize the move of God to bring Gentiles into the kingdom. The poetic image

---

3. The citation comes from the Greek version of Isaiah 53:7–8.
4. The citation comes from Amos 9:11–12.
5. The citation comes from Isaiah 45:21.

revolves around the notion that David's collapsed tent (i.e., the fallen kingdom) would be restored to such an extent that even the Gentiles would find God's presence therein.

Finding the Unknown God (17:23–31)

> 23 As for the inscription "To an Unknown God,"
> I have come here to tell you the One who is divine—
> 24 it is the God who created the universe and every living thing;
> he is Lord of all the heavens and earth.
> 25 Too magnificent to dwell in man-made temples,
> he does not need anything, much less the service our hands.
>
> This God, who breathes life into all he makes,
> 26 created from one man every nation
> spread across the face of the earth,
> where each lives for certain seasons
> in various lands bounded by oceans.
>
> 27 They were created to seek this God,
> even grope for him, until they find him,
> even though the Divine exists not far from any of us—
> 28 since in him we live and move and have our being.
> And as yet another poet wrote: we are his offspring.[6]

---

6. The line "in him we live and move and have our being" comes from Epimenides (c. 600 BC), Cretica. The line "we are his offspring" comes from Aratus (c. 315–240 BC), Phenomena 5 (which at the beginning has *ek Dios archomestha* = we had our beginning from God) or Cleanthes (331–233 BC), Hymn to Zeus 4 (ek sou gar genos semen). Paul also quoted one line from the same poem (and stanza) of Epimenides in Titus 1:12, "Cretans [are] always liars, evil beasts, idle bellies." According to a Syriac version (see F. F. Bruce, *Acts of the Apostles*, 384), the stanza

29 Since we are God's offspring,
we ought not to think that deity is like anything
man could make from gold, silver, or stone.
30 The Divine cannot be captured by the imagination
of even the most skilled cratsman.

God overlooked this ignorance in the past,
but now he is proclaiming that all people
should change their thinking while there is time,
31 for God has set a day for all earth's inhabitants
to be judged by one appointed man
whom God raised from the dead.

---

reads: "They fashioned a tomb for you, high and holy One—/the Cretans, always liars, evil beasts, idle bellies!—/but you are not dead; you are risen and living,/for in you we live and move and have our being."

6

The Epistles of Paul

Encomium for Christ's Love (Rom 8:28–39)

28 God turns everything to good
for those who love him and are called by him
    to know his designs. God has planned
29 the destiny of those he's always known—
    they'll become like his Son, the first perfect man.
30 Their horizons have been determined by God
    who makes all things right for those he loves
and promises to bring them into his glory!

31 What, then, can we say about the pains of this life?
If God is our advocate, who can be our enemy?
32 This is the God who did not spare his own Son
    but for our sake sacrificed him.
This is the God who lavishes us with all goodness,
    the God who has given us his Son.

33 Who can level any accusation against God's chosen ones,
    when God is the one who stands by us?

34 Who can posit any condemnation against us
    when Christ Jesus experienced crucifixion
on our behalf, then rose again to appear before God,
    pleading our cause day and night.

35 Who can rip us away from Christ's love?
    Can the sword of affliction or distress?
Can persecution or famine? Nakedness or peril?
    As it is written in the scriptures,
36 *For your sake, we are killed all day long.*
    We are nothing more than sheep for slaughter.[1]

37 But in all these things we are super-conquerers
    through Christ who loves us.
38 For I am persuaded there's nothing in death or life
    that can rip us away from God's love
39 because we are held firm by Jesus Christ our Lord.
    No angel, ruler, power, or creature can separate us!
No matter how high or low we go, we are held by our Lord.

This passage is poetic by virtue of its exultant language—triumphant in the face of trial. The structure is also poetic in that the entire text moves along by a series of rhetorical questions. The penultimate stanza is the most vivid, presenting several concrete images of affliction. The last stanza celebrates Christ's all-embracing, all-powerful love.

Promises for the Gentiles and the Jews (Rom 9:24–33)

24 God's calling is not just to the Jews
    but also to the Gentiles.
25 This is as Hosea says,

Those who were not my people,
    I will call "my people."
She who was not loved
    will become my beloved.

1. The citation comes from Psalm 44:22.

26 *Instead of being named "not my people,"*
    they will be called "children of the living God."[2]
27 Isaiah laments for Israel,

Though the children of Israel are as innumerable
    as the sand on the seashore, only a few will be rescued.
28 *Without any hesitation or delay*
    the Lord will execute his judgment on earth.

29 Isaiah predicted this before:

If the Lord of heaven's armies had not left any survivors,
we would have become as desolate as Sodom and Gomorrah.[3]

30 Is it possible that the Gentiles
not striving for righteousness,
have found a good standing by faith?
31 And that Israel, striving for righteousness
based on the law, did not find it
32 because it was done by works, not faith?

They tripped over the stumbling stone,
33 Just as it was written,

In Zion I place a stone they stumble over,
    a rock that causes people to trip.
And *those who place their trust in him*
    will never be dismayed.[4]

---

2. The two citations come from Hosea 2:23; 1:10.

3. The two citations come from the Greek version of Isaiah 10:22–23; 1:9.

4. These two quotations come from the Greek version of Isaiah 8:14; 28:16.

This pastiche has a combination of OT poems to speak of the fact that the majority of Jews rejected Jesus as the Messiah, while a few (the remnant) accepted him. This pastiche is very similar to that found in 1 Peter 2:4–10. Both share several of the same verses: Isaiah 8:14; 28:16; Hosea 1:9–10; 2:23. In both works, the major thesis is that the Jews forfeited being God's people (except for a remnant in the Roman's version) by stumbling over the rock (Jesus Christ) and were therefore replaced by Gentiles who place their trust in him. The fact that both Paul and Peter used these verses strongly suggests that these passages were part of what is known as "Testimonia," collections of OT verses used to substantiate the claims of early Christians.

The Vastness of the Lord (Rom 11:33–36)

33 How deep is God's wealth, wisdom, and knowledge!
How unsearchable are his decisions!
How untraceable are his ways!

34 *Who has ever understood the Lord's thoughts?*
Who could ever become his advisor?[5]
35 *Who can give him anything he doesn't already have?*[6]
36 Everything comes from him, goes through him, and is for him,
who receives the glory into everlasting ages. Amen.

This poetic outburst praises God for his profound wisdom, his unsearchable ways, and omnipotence. It is the only NT passage to cite a verse from Job.

---

5. The citation comes from the Greek version of Isaiah 40:13.
6. The citation comes from Job 41:11.

The Root of Jesse Praised by Gentiles (Rom 15:9–13)

9 The Gentiles will glorify God for his mercy,
as was promised in the Scriptures:

I will praise you among the Gentiles;
 I will sing psalms exulting God's Name.
10 The Gentiles will rejoice in God,
 along with the people of Israel.
11 All the Gentiles will praise the Lord—
 all nations will extol him!

This is as Isaiah said,

12 The Root of Jesse will sprout—
he will rise to rule the Gentiles,
 who will put their hopes in him.

13 May the God who gives you hope
 fill you with all joy, peace, and faith!
May your hope abound,
empowered by the sacred Spirit!

This poem is a pastiche put together from the following OT verses: v. 9 from Psalm 18:49; v. 10 from Deuteronomy 32:43; v. 11 from Psalm 117:1; v. 12 from the Greek version of Isaiah 11:10. The last stanza of the poem is a doxology.

Doxology Praising Christ (Rom 16:25–27)

25 Praise God who has the power to strengthen you
according to my gospel
and the proclamation of Jesus Christ,
according to the unveiling of the mystery
 which lay silent through the epochs

26 but is now proclaimed to the Gentiles,
   as revealed through the prophetic writings,
   for them to know it, believe, and obey—
according to the command of the eternal God.

27 Praise God, unique and sagacious.
To Jesus Christ be glory through everlasting ages.

As in many doxologies, Paul elevated his language beyond normal prose into poetry. This poetic doxology is syntactically balanced by the three-time occurrence of the Greek preposition *kata* (translated here as "according to").

Creed of Monotheism (1 Cor 8:6)

There is one God, the Father,
who is the source of all—
   we live in him.
There is one Lord, Jesus Christ,
who is the course of all—
   we live through him.

An alternative, literal rendering shows the poetic structure in the Greek better:

There is one God, the Father
   of whom are all things
      and we in him,
   and one Lord, Jesus Christ
      through whom are all things
         and we through him.

The idea is that the Father is the source and the Lord Jesus is the course (way). The poetic structure of the creed enhanced memorization.

The Supremacy of Love (1 Cor 13)

1 If I could speak all the languages
used by men and angels,
but do not express love,
I am a noisy gong, a clanging cymbal.

2 If I could prophecy about all the mysteries,
and have faith to move mountains,
but do not know love,
I am nothing.

3 If I give away everything I own
and surrender my body to martyrdom,
but do not give love,
I cannot boast I've done anything.[7]

4 Love is longsuffering and love is kind.
Love is not jealous, boastful, or conceited.
5 Love is not pretentious[8] or self-seeking.
Love is not irritable or resentful.
6 Love, unhappy with injustice, is pleased with truth.
7 Love is all-enduring, all-believing,
ever hopeful, and ever steadfast.

---

7. This translates the variant reading which literally reads, "if I give my body that I may boast" (*kauchesomai*), supported by the earliest manuscripts (P46 ℵ A B). I understand the giving of one's body to probably indicate martyrdom. Another variant reading in later manuscripts has the word *kauthesomai* (I may burn)—"If I give my body that I may burn." Martyrdom via burning at the stake did not happen until about 10 years after Paul wrote 1 Corinthians, during Nero's persecution of Christians in Rome

8. This translates the variant reading of P46, *ouk euschemonei*.

8 Love never fails.
Prophecies will vanish, tongues will fall silent,
and our knowledge will fade away.
9 We know imperfectly and prophecy imperfectly.
10 But when the eschaton comes,
we will be done with imperfection.

11 When I was a child, I talked like a child,
thought like a child, and reasoned like a child.
When I became a man, I stopped my childish ways.

12 As for now, we see mere reflections in a mirror,
but then, we will see clearly, face to face.
As for now, my knowledge is imperfect,
but then, I will fully know, even as I was fully known.

13 Three things will always remain:
faith, hope, and love.
The most supreme is love.

1 Corinthians 13 is a powerful poem, not just in 13:1–7 or 13:4–7, as is recognized by several English versions, but in its entirety. Therefore, I have presented the entire chapter as a poem.

The Resurrection (1 Cor 15:35–57)

35 You ask, "How are the dead raised
and with what kind of body do they come?"

36 Seed does not sprout unless it dies.
37 The form it grows is not what is sown
but a different shape than the bare grain.
Just as every seed grows into a distinct form,

38 God gives risen ones the kind of body he desires.

39 Not all creatures have the same kind of body,
as can be seen in men, animals, birds, and fish,
40 which have earthly bodies unlike those from heaven.
Each of these possess their unique glory,
just as the celestial bodies shining over earth—
41 the sun has its splendor, as do the moon and stars,
which differ with one another in how they shine.

42 And so it is with the resurrection body.
What is sown always decays, what is raised never fades.
43 It is sown in dishonor and raised in splendor.
It is sown in weakness and raised in power.
44 It is sown as a natural body and raised a spiritual body.
Since there is a body for our earthly soul,
45 there will also be a spiritual—for it is written,
the first man Adam became a living soul;[9]
the last Adam became life-giving Spirit.

46 First the natural body, afterward the spiritual.
47 The first man was made of the dust of the earth.
The second man is made of heaven.
48 Those born of the first man are no more than dust.
Those born of the heavenly man are celestial.
49 As we carried the image of the man of dust,
we will also express the image of the heavenly man.

50 Flesh and blood cannot inherit God's kingdom,
nor can the perishable inherit immortality.
51 But there is a mystery awaiting us:
we will not all die, but we will all be changed—

---

9. The citation comes from Genesis 2:7.

52 in an instant, in the blink of an eye—
when the last trumpet sounds, we will be changed;
the dead will rise into immortality.

53–54 When the perishable becomes imperishable
and the mortal immortal, then this word will be fulfilled:

Death has been swallowed up! Victory![10]
55 *Where is your victory, O death!? Where is your sting?*[11]

56 The sting of death is sin—empowered by the law.
57 But God has given us victory over sin and death
through the conqueror, our Lord Jesus Christ!

The resurrection life, an abstract idea, is poetically expressed via images of seeds and plants, earthly bodies of various earthly creatures, and celestial bodies expressing varying degrees of splendor. The final victory over death is presented through many abstractions (immortality, imperishable, etc.) and a few concrete images—transfiguration happens "in the blink of an eye" when death "will be swallowed up."

Prayer for Enlightening and Empowering (Eph 1:17–23)

17 May the God of our Lord Jesus Christ,
the glorious Father, illumine your spirit
with wisdom and revelation
so that you might really know him!

---

10. The citation comes from Isaiah 25:8.
11. The citation comes from the Greek version of Hosea 13:14.

> 18 May your spiritual eyes be enlightened
> so you might fully understand
> that he has called to you to participate
> in his splendid spiritual wealth—
> a hope turned into actual inheritance!
>
> 19 May we experience the supernatural strength
> of his power to us who believe—
> for this was the mighty power God exerted
> 20 in raising Christ from the dead
> and enthroning him in heaven's zenith
> 21 above every ruler, authority, power, and lord,
> bestowing on him a name above all,
> not only in this age but in the one to come,
> 22 subordinating everything under his feet
> and appointing him the Supreme over everything
> 23 in the church, which is his body on earth,
> the fullness of the One who fills all with his all.

This poetic prayer has all the earmarks of being a carefully crafted composition as opposed to a spontaneous utterance. In the Greek, the prayer is just one sentence (which actually begins in 1:15), wherein Paul asks God to give the believers a fuller knowledge of him (God) via spiritual enlightenment (stanza 1). This is followed by three items (signaled in Greek by *ti* = "what is") that contribute to the fuller knowledge: (1) knowing the hope of the Christian calling and (2) the riches of God's inheritance in the believers (stanza 1), as well as (3) experientially knowing the greatness of God's power accessible to the believer—a power he exerted in raising Christ from the dead, seating him in the heavenlies, and making him head over all things to the church, which is the embodied expression of him who fills all with his all (stanza 3).

Prayer for Experiencing Christ's Indwelling (Eph 3:14-21)

> 14 For this reason I bend my knees to the Father
> > 15 who has families scattered in heaven and earth.
>
> 16 I pray he may grant you according to his glorious riches
> > to be mightily empowered in your inner being
> > 17 by his Spirit, so as to experience Christ's indwelling,
> > giving you rooting and founding in love,
> > 18 mightily strengthening you all together
> > to grasp the breadth, length, height, and depth—
> > 19 to know the knowledge-surpassing love of Christ,
>
> so that you might be filled to overflowing with all the fullness of God.
>
> 20 To him who is able to make all things happen
> > way beyond what we ask or think
> > because he gives us the exceeding power.
>
> 21 To him be glory in Christian gatherings and in Christ Jesus
>
> for all generations, for ages to come.

Paul intended to offer the prayer at the beginning of chpt. 3, broke off with a discourse about his knowledge of the mystery of Christ, and then commenced his prayer in 3:14. As such, it has the appearance of being spoken spontaneously. This is possible. But it is also possible that he had the poem written out before him and was about to read it to his amanuensis, when he digressed. Either way, this prayer, as with the previous one, was a carefully crafted composition. Paul bends his knees to the Father of the universe and then offers one of the most grandiose prayers in the Bible. The poem in Greek is structured symmetrically by one *hina* clause ("I pray that") followed by two aorist infinitives ("to be mightily empowered" and "to experience Christ's indwelling"), then another *hina* clause ("so that you will be able") followed by two aorist infinitives ("to grasp the breadth, etc." and "to know . . . the love of Christ"), then a final *hina* clause ("so that you might be filled to overflowing"). I have reflected this structure in the English translation. The poem concludes with a glowing doxology in the last stanza.

Creed of Christian Unity (Eph 4:4–6)

> 4 There is one community and one common Spirit,
> and we are called by God to share one hope.
> 5 There is one Lord, one faith, one baptism,
> 6 one God and Father of all,
> who is transcendent, pervasive, and immanent.

Novum Testamentum Graece (27th edition) sets verses 5 and 6 as poetry, but not verse 4, probably because the editors thought only these verses comprise the creed, not v. 4. However, v. 4 shares the same structure and lexical features as the other verses, and belongs in the poem. This passage "has the nature of an early Christian credo, not unprecedented in the Pauline writings, but more elaborate than its predecessors"—e.g., 1 Cor 8:6 (F. F. Bruce, *Ephesians,* 335). The wording in Ephesians 4:4–6 is built around "one Spirit, one Lord, one God."

Early Christian Poem (Eph 5:14)

> O sleeping one,
> wake up from the dead,
> and Christ's light will dawn[12] on you.

This three-line poem, known as a tristich, has a metrical rhythm that was especially associated with religious initiation chants. It is likely that early Christians adapted the rhythm for Christian initiation rite of baptism; the wording is loosely based on Isaiah 60:1. The expressions "wake up" and "rise from the dead" are clearly resurrectional; resurrection and baptism were closely linked in the early church (see Rom 6:3–4; see Wood, "Ephesians," 70–71 in the *Expositor's Bible Commentary*). The hymn could possibly be one of the hymns or spiritual songs Paul speaks of a few verses later (5:18).

There is another version of this hymn in the third line according to certain manuscripts and witnesses (D it[b] Victorinus, Ambrosiaster, Jerome):

> O sleeping one,
> wake up from the dead,
> and Christ will touch you.

In his *Commentary on Ephesians* (PL 26, 559a), Jerome interprets the words as addressed by Christ to Adam when releasing him from Hades. Jerome said that Adam was held prisoner directly beneath the place where Christ was crucified, the name Golgotha being derived from Adam's skull, which was thought to be buried there.

---

12. The Greek verb *epiphosko* is used in Matt 28:1 and Luke 23:54 for the dawning of a new day (which was the day of Jesus' resurrection).

The Incarnate Christ (Phil 2:5-11)

5-6 Though he was living as God in divine form,[13]
 Christ Jesus chose not to cling to his equality with God[14]

13. "Living as God in divine form," is literally "who existing in God's form." The Greek doesn't say, "he was God," nor does it say he was "the form of God." Rather, it says that he was existing *in* God's form. "God's form" in Greek is *morphe theou*. "*Morphe* always signifies a form which truly and fully expresses the being which underlies it" (Moulton and Milligan, *The Vocabulary of the Greek New Testament*, 417). It is what gives expression to an essence. A man—with his body, mind, as soul—expresses the essence of humanity. A human lives in *morphe anthropou*—that is, in human expression. One who is God lives in *morphe theou*—that is, in divine expression. Another way to say this is that *morphe* denotes one's mode of being in the sense that *morphe* is that which truly characterizes a given reality—those characters and qualities that are essential to any given being (Fee, *Philippians*, 204). Because Christ existed as God, "his true nature is characterized not by selfish grabbing, but by an open-handed giving" (Hawthorne, *Philippians*, 85).

14. "Chose not to cling to his equality with God." Literally, "he did not consider the [his] being all things equal to God as something to be grasped." This statement explains what it is for Christ to be "in God's form." As one existing in God's form, he is all things equal to God. The word behind "cling" is *harpagmon*, a noun denoting grasping. This "grasping" can be understood in three basic ways: (1) "trying to attain," "grasping so as to get"; (2) "clinging to," "retaining," "holding on to"; (3) "an opportunity for grasping." The first option can be ruled out by context—namely, Christ already existed in God's form (as God), so there were would be no cause for him to want to grasp after this. In other words, he wasn't seeking God-likeness, because he was already God. The second option does work in the context, for it denotes that Christ, being all things equal with God, could have insisted on his equality with God and not taken a servant's role. As an equal, he had this prerogative. He could have clung to his equality. Had he insisted on retaining/grasping to this equality, he would not have become the suffering Servant, the redeemer. The third option denotes that Christ did not consider his equality with God as providing him with an opportunity for grasping—that is, as a matter of seizing upon this equality to his own advantage. Christ

7 but rather poured himself out[15] into a servant's life
> by being born in the likeness of men.

And being found among men as man
> 8 he humbled himself in human servitude,

becoming obedient even unto death,
> and that, a death by crucifixion.

9 Because of this, God exalted him,
> giving him the Name above every other.

10 Every knee should bend to Jesus.
> Every creature in heaven, on earth,
>> 11 and under earth—every creature with a tongue—

should confess, "the Lord is Jesus Christ"
> to God the Father's glory.

The poem has two major strophes: 2:6–8 (the humiliation of Christ) and 2:9–11 (the exaltation of Christ). The passage is widely regarded as an early hymn (or what I would call a poem—see following discussion) about Christ's preexis-

---

did not consider being equal with God as something to be taken selfish advantage of, something to further his own ends. Equality with God did not mean for Christ to be a grasping, seizing being, as it would be for the gods and lords whom the Philippians had previously known. The normal expectation of godly/lordly power is to seize, to grasp, to take all things for themselves. Contrarily, Christ expressed his equality with God when he emptied himself (Fee, *Philippians*, 207–209; Comfort, *Philippians*, 168–180).

15. the Greek term for "poured himself out" is *heauton ekenosen* (lit. "he emptied himself"). The text does not say that he emptied himself of anything in particular; it simply says he emptied himself. It is possible that emptying himself is tantamount to pouring himself out—so Hawthorne (*Philippians*, 86), who wrote, "it is a poetic, humanlike way of saying that Christ poured out himself, putting himself totally at the disposal of people (cf. 1 John 3:16), that Christ became poor that he might make many rich (2 Cor 8:9)."

tence and divine nature, incarnation and death, exaltation and Lordship. Whether the passage is to be understood as a (1) pre-Pauline hymn (i.e., a hymn Paul borrowed) or (2) a hymn composed by Paul has been debated by scholars and continues to be debated. O'Brien (*Philippians*, 188–193) and Fee (*Philippians*, 191–194) present excellent discussions on the issue. It is possible that Paul borrowed a preexistent hymn. We know that when the early Christians gathered together they sang OT psalms, as well as hymns and spiritual songs (Eph 5:19; Col 3:16). The latter two—"hymns and spiritual songs"—must have been creations of the early Christians. Philippians 2:6–11 may have been such a hymn that Paul adapted for use in this letter. Even if Paul did adapt this hymn, we must consider him to be its ultimate author in that he dictated this hymn to his amanuensis (see Fee op. cit., 193) and thereby gave it its final written form, the words we now read in 2:6–11.

However, it seems far more likely that Philippians 2:6–11 is a poem composed by Paul. This view is strongly supported by the fact that there are very strong lexical ties between Philippians 2:6–11 and Philippians 3:20–21 (see notes on next poem). Since Paul was clearly the author of the verses in chapter 3, it stands to reason that he authored the passage in chapter 2. And if he wrote this afresh for the Philippians, he was giving them a poem, not a hymn. Other portions of Paul's writings exhibit his poetic ability, such as the encomium for Christ's love (Rom 8:38–39), the doxology praising Christ (Rom 16:25–27), the poetic prayer (Eph 3:14–21), the love poem (1 Cor 13:4–6), the poem about the preeminent Christ (Col 1:15–20), and two poems for Christ's epiphany (1 Tim 6:15–16; Titus 3:4–7). All of these passages display poetic language, cadence, and majesty, setting them apart even from exalted prose. In short, Paul became poetic on occasion. And Philippians 2:6–11 is one of his brilliant masterpieces.

A more filled-out rendering of this poem is as follows:

He was God in nature, form, and mode of being.
He was everything God was with all divine privilege.
Yet he did not cling to this divine equality
or use it for his own advantage
like some god grasping for more.
Rather, he emptied himself by pouring out himself
into the form of a slave, a servant of divine will.
He was born human with flesh, bone, and blood
and looked every much man except he was also God.
People saw him as man, as one of them,
as he humbled himself to the Father's mind,
and became obedient,
even when that led to humiliating death by crucifixion.

Having abandoned himself to ultimate sacrifice,
the Father did not abandon him.
Rather, he lifted him, exalted him,
and graced him with preeminence,
giving him the Name above every other in this universe,
so that at the name of Jesus every knee should bow
and every tongue—in heaven, on earth, or under earth—
should openly confess with praise: "the Lord is Jesus Christ!"
to the glory of his Father.

Heavenly Citizenship (Phil 3:20-21)

> Our citizenship exists in the heavens
> from where also we eagerly expect
> the Savior, the Lord Jesus Christ
> who will transfigure our humiliating bodies
> that they may be like his glorious body
> by the power that enables him
> to subject all things to himself.

The lexical similarities between Philippians 2:6–11 and 3:20–21 strongly suggest they were composed by the same author, who had to have been Paul. This reinforces what I affirmed for the previous poem: Paul was the original composer; he was not exerpting an existing Christian hymn (see Comfort, *Philippians*, 209–211).

The Preeminent Christ (Col 1:12-20)

> 12 We thank you, our Father, for qualifying us
>   to enjoy a portion of the inheritance of every saint,
>   to partake of your marvelous Son who lives in light.
> 13 For you have rescued us from dread darkness
>   and transferred us into a brilliant kingdom
>   where we glory in the Son of your love.
> 14 In him we have redemption, the forgiveness of our sins.
>
> 15 He is the visage of the invisible God,
> the premier over all creation,[16]

---

16. In Greek this is *prototokos pases ktiseos*. Though *prototokos* literally means "firstborn," the sense is often simply "first one" or "premier" without any idea of "born" as such (see BAGD, 726). The genitive *pases ktiseos* is not a genitive of inclusion ("first/premier of/among all creation"), but a genitive of distinction: "premier over all creation"—this

16 because every living thing was created in him—
> the visible creatures on earth
> and invisible beings in the heavens,
> such as angelic thrones, lords, rulers, and powers.

17 All things through him and for him have been created.
While he himself exists before all things,
> their existence is held together by his presence.

18 In every way he has become premier;
He is fountainhead of the body, the church's source.
He is our beginning by being death's firstborn.

19 God's Fullness is pleased to reside in Christ
20 through whom God will recover everything to himself—
> every single creature in heaven and on earth—
because Jesus made peace for the universe
> by shedding his blood on the cross.

This passage stands out as one of Paul's most sublime poetic creations. It celebrates the Son of God's preeminence with respect to creation (concerning which he is the premier via his role as creator and sustainer) and to the new creation, the church (concerning which he is the premier via his role as the first to rise from the dead and the church's fountainhead). As both, he is God's fullness, whose ultimate function is to be the mediator of God's recovery of the entire universe.

---

sense being determined by the next lines which declare the Son's divine participation in the creation of everything and his existence prior to creation.

The Eternal King (1 Tim 1:17)

> Honor and glory to the eternal King!
> He alone is the indestructible, invisible God!
> May his reign be everlasting!

Paul's praise of Christ's mercy and grace led quite naturally to this doxology. "He is the King eternal" is literally "to the King of the ages." This reflects a Jewish view of history as "this age" and "the age to come." The Greek behind "indestructible" is *aphthartos*; it denotes that which cannot be corrupted and does not perish. Greek philosophers applied this characteristic to the soul (as opposed to the body). "Invisible" means that which cannot be seen with the mortal eye (*a* + *horatos*; cf. Col 1:15 above). The statement "he alone is God" (lit. "the only God") is distinctively Jewish (as opposed to the polytheism of the non-Jewish world).

Hymnal Creed of Christ, the Mediator (1 Tim 2:3–6)

> 3 What is excellent and pleasing to God our Savior
> 4 is that people are saved and know this truth:
> > 5 There is one God and one mediator
> > between God and men, the man Christ Jesus,
> > 6 who offered himself as a ransom for all
> > through martyrdom, at just the right time.

Verses 5–6 comprise a creedal hymn, which was likely memorized and recited by early Christians. The creed contains two fundamental truths of Judaism and Christianity: there is "one God" and there is "one mediator." "One God" is the central theological tenet of Judaism. The Shema begins by affirming "Hear O Israel, the Lord our God, the

Lord is one" (Deut 6:4). This stands in stark opposition to the polytheism of Israel's neighbors and interjects a note of absolute exclusivity. The expression "one mediator, Christ Jesus" indicates that God created everything in heaven and on earth through Christ (Col 1:16) and then reconciled it all to himself through Christ (2 Cor 5:18).

Creedal Hymn of the Mystery of Godliness (1 Tim 3:16)

> We confess the sacred mystery:
>
> He was manifested in the flesh.
> > He was justified in spirit.
> He was seen by angels.
> > He was proclaimed among nations.
> He was believed in the world.
> > He was taken up in glory.

In the Greek, this passage is immediately recognizable as a poem, which was very likely sung as a creedal hymn. Each line is structured the same: a passive voice verb (each ending in theta/eta), followed by the proposition *en*, followed by a noun in the dative case. The beauty of the poem is that readers can read it as a pithy chronology of Jesus' life and ministry from the first line to the last (manifested in flesh ... taken up in glory), or each of the three couplets can be read as *first* presenting Jesus' life on earth, followed by post-resurrection realities (1a, 1b; 2a, 2b; 3a, 3b):

1a manifested in flesh (via incarnation)
2a seen by angels (after his birth, in the wilderness, garden of Gethsemane)
3a believed (by some) in this world

followed by his life after death and resurrection:
> 1b justified in spirit (via his resurrection into spiritual life)
> 2b proclaimed among nations (by the apostles and so on)
> 3b taken up in glory (his present exultant state)

Christ's Epiphany (1 Tim 6:14–16)

> 14 Keep the faith until the epiphany of Jesus Christ
>   who will be revealed when the time has come.
> 15 He is the blessed One and only Sovereign,
>   the King of kings, the Lord of lords,
> 16 the only One having immortality
>   inhabiting light inaccesible to mortals
>   which no one has seen or ever can—
> to him be eternal honor and power! Amen.

This poetic passage emerges out the midst of Paul's final exhortations to Timothy. The second stanza of Paul's encomia of Christ's epiphany simulates language of the hymns of praise in the Psalter (Ps 136:3) and applies it to Christ (so also Rev 17:14). The third stanza has the richest language, wherein Paul exalts Christ as the only one who has "immortality" (the Greek term is an alpha private plus *thanatos* – *athanatos*, the negation of death). The confession that Christ alone is intrinsically immortal is found only here in the NT. His immortality is magnified by the fact that mere mortals cannot access the light he inhabits and cannot see him (cf. Exod 33:20; John 1:18). His epiphany contrasts with Greek mythology where so-called immortal gods made epiphanies.

Suffering for Christ's Gospel (2 Tim 1:8–10)

8 Suffer for the cause of the gospel
    by being empowered by God,
9 who saved us and called us to a sacred vocation
    not according to our deeds
    but according to his own design and kindness,
which he gave us in Christ Jesus
    before everlasting ages
10 and is now revealed through the epiphany
of our Savior Christ Jesus,
    who snuffed out death
    and lit the path to amarathine life.

This poem springs out of another exhortation (see previous poem) from Paul to Timothy. As in the previous poem, the mention of Christ's epiphany sparked exalted language, especially in the last stanza. I used the phrases "snuffed out death" and "lit the path to amarathine" to highlight the contrast. The Greek participle behind "snuffed out" (*katargeo*) has the sense of "abolish, wipe out" (see 1 Cor 15:26, 53–54; 2 Thess 2:8; Heb 2:14). The phrase "lit the path" translates the aorist participle *photisantos*, from *photizo*, "bring to light," "reveal" (cf. Eph 3:9). The line is literally, "brought life and incorruptibility to light." The words "life" and "incorruptibility" form a single idea: "life incorruptible," which I think is more felicitously translated as "amarathine life." The two words form a hendiadys, a literary device wherein a single idea is expressed by means of two words joined by "and."

The "Saying" of Faithfulness (2 Tim 2:11–13)

11 This is a trustworthy saying:
if we die with Christ, we will live with him;
12 if we endure, we will be kings with him;
if we will deny him, he will deny us;
13 if we are faithless, he will remain faithful,
  for he cannot deny himself.

This poem is one of the "sayings" found in the Pastoral Epistles which came from the early church. The poetic nature of the saying is immediately apparent in the Greek by the uniform structuring of every line (which appears to be typical of Hebrew poetic parallelism), as well as the pithy, profound vocabulary. This wording aided memorization, whether for recitation or singing. The Greek verb in the first phrase of the second line (*sunapethanomen*) can be understood literally, metaphorically, or spiritually—or comprehensively. The tense could also be understood as referring to the believer's participation in Christ's historic death ("we died with him"; cf. Rom 6:1–4). The same ambiguity surrounds the statement "we will also live with him" (*suzesomen*). Both statements, being poetic, are open ended. The next line speaks of endurance as a necessary qualification for reigning with Christ (*sumbasileusomen*). (Note the three Greek words all beginning with sun/sum, meaning "together with," or "union.") In the next statement ("if we will deny him, he will deny us"), the verb shifts to a Greek future tense (*arnesometha*) completing the progression within the series of protases (*if* clauses): aorist (died), present (endure), future (will deny). This line is reminiscent of Jesus' poetic saying in Matthew 10:33 (cf. Mark 8:38; Luke 12:9).

The "Saying" of the Savior's Epiphany (Titus 3:4–8a)

4–5 Not because of righteous works we have done,
but by his mercy, God our Savior rescued us.
His epiphany came with love and kindness.

He lavishly poured his sacred Spirit upon us.
6 This Spirit regenerates, renews, and washes—
thanks to the grace of Jesus Christ our Savior
7 who made us right with God and heirs of eternal life.

8 We can count on this trustworthy saying.

This is another of the trustworthy sayings in the Pastoral Epistles; it is coupled with yet another celebration of the Savior's epiphany, especially in terms of what he gave each believer through the Spirit's regeneration, renewal, and washing. "Regeneration" translates *palingenesia*, which is used for cosmic renewal (after the flood – 1 Clement 9:4; in the future age of the Messiah – Matt 19:28), or for the experience of a complete change of life ("re-genesis"). This and Matthew 19:28 are the only NT uses of this word. The word was used widely in the ancient world for many different kinds of renewal. Its use in Titus 3:5 probably refers to the individual's incorporation into the cosmic renewal with a view to its future completion. Paul also calls this regeneration a "renewing."

7

The Epistle to the Hebrews

Prologue Poem to the Superior Son (1:1–13)

1 In multiple portions and multifarious ways,
the God who spoke to our ancestors through prophets,
2–3 has, in these last days, spoken to us in the Son
    who is the radiant aura of God's glory,
    the presentation of God's essence,
    and sustainer of everything by his potent word.
The Son, who spoke the universal ages into being,
    is the heir of all that is yet to come;
    having purified the world of sin,
    he is now sitting at the Majesty's right hand.

4 The Son is vastly superior to all the angels,
as the Name he's honored with is far better than theirs.
5 For to which of the angels did God ever say,
    You are my Son;
    today I have become your Father.
And again,
    I will be his Father and he will be my son.
6 And again,
    when he brings his firstborn into the heavenly sphere,
    God says, "let all my angels revere him."

7 In speaking of the angels he says,
> *"I make my angels winds*
> *and my servants flickering flames."*

8 But about his Son, God says,
> *"Your throne, O God, will last for ever and ever*
> *because justice is the sceptre of your kingdom.*
> *9 You have loved what's right and hated evil;*
> *therefore, O God, your God has gladly anointed you*
> *over and above your angelic companions."*

10 God also says to the Son,
> *"In the beginning, O Lord, you founded the earth,*
> > *and the heavens were made by your hands.*
> *11 They will unravel, but you remain forever;*
> *they will get old like worn clothes.*
> *12 You will roll them up like a robe;*
> *like a garment they will be changed.*
> *But you always are; your years will never end."*

13 But to which of the angels did God ever say,
> *"Sit at my right hand until I make*
> *your enemies a footstool for your feet"?**

Novum Testamentum Graece (27th edition) sets the first chapter of Hebrews in poetic format, but doesn't begin the poem until verse 3. I think the poem begins in 1:1. Note the rhythmical balance between 1:1 and 1:2:

A In multiple portions and multifarious ways
B God spoke through the prophets to our ancestors;
A' in these last days
B' he has spoken to us in the Son.

The first line of the first stanza mirrors the alliteration of the words *polumeros* (meaning "many shares, allotments, portions") and *polutropos* (meaning "many ways"—varied, diverse). The poetic description of the Son begins thereafter. Two of the most succinct and sublime expressions of the Son's eternal being are found in the words "the radiant aura of God's glory" (*apaugasma tes doxes*) and "the presentation of God's essence" (*charakter tes hupostaseos*).

After the first stanza, the rest of the poem is a pastiche taken from the following OT verses: v. 5 from Psalm 2:7; 2 Samuel 7:14; v. 6 from the Greek version of Deuteronomy 32:43; v. 7 from the Greek version of Psalm 104:4; vv. 8–9 from Psalm 45:6–7; vv. 10–12 from the Greek version of Psalm 105:25–27; v. 13 from Psalm 110:1.

The Panegyric (12:18–24)

18 You have not come to something that can be touched,
  or felt the blazing fire—the gloom, storm, darkness.
19 You have not come to something that can be heard:
   the trumpet call and the dreadful voice
   that people begged to hear no more, for it was said,
   20 "if even an animal touches the mountain
   it has to be stoned to death."

  21 So frightful was the appearing—like a phantom—
  that Moses trembling cried, "I am terrified!"

22 You have come to Mount Zion,
   to the city of the living God, the heavenly Jerusalem;
   to the panegyric of myriad angels,
   23 to the gathering of all the firstborn enrolled in heaven,

> to the spirits of righteous people who've been perfected;
> you have come to God who is the judge of everyone
> 24 and to Jesus who is the mediator of the new covenant
> inaugurated by his sprinkled blood,
> which speaks so much better than Abel's.

This poem vividly contrasts the frightening situation in the first OT gathering (when God met with the people to give them the Decalogue—see Exod 19) with the pleasant situation in the new covenant gathering or what is called "the panegyric"—a term that was used by Greeks to describe a festal gathering. The contrast is set between what could not be touched (or, approached) because it was all so frightening and what can now be touched (or, approached) because God has graciously made himself available to his people through Christ. The poem is structured with two contrasting stanzas (two sentences in Greek). The first stanza poeticizes the things the people of the new covenant did not have to experience as did those who first received the giving of the law, while the second stanza poeticizes ten things the people of the new covenant can experience.

Doxology of Praise (13:20–21)

> 20–21 May the God of peace supply you
> with everything you need to do his will
> and live in a way that pleases him.
>
> Our God raised our Lord Jesus from the dead—
> he is the Shepherd of the sheep,
> whose blood bought an everlasting covenant for us.
>
> All glory belongs to him forever and ever. Amen.

In Greek this doxology is so lexically loaded that the writer had difficulty maintaining smooth syntax. In the English translation I have straightened this out somewhat. The mention of the risen Jesus Christ followed by the strange juxtaposition of him being both shepherd and lamb (implied by the mention of blood sacrifice) makes for stunning poetry.

8

The Epistle of James

The Destiny of the Rich (1:9–11)

9 Let the humble boast of their exaltation,
10 and the wealthy of their humiliation—
because they will pass away
like the flowers in the meadow.

11 When the sun rises, it whips up a scorching wind
withering wild flowers, killing their blossomed beauty.
It is the same with the rich who drop dead
just when they think they're getting ahead.

The message (and poetic image) in the first stanza draws upon verses like Psalm 49:16–17. The image in the second stanza is like that found in Hosea 13:15, which speaks of the east wind rising and scorching proud Ephraim who had sprung up like a flower in the desert. The eastern sun rising in the desert brings a scorching wind.

The Father of Lights (1:17–18)

17 All that is good and perfect is given to us from above—
it comes down to us from the Father of all light,
with whom there is no variation or turning of the shadow.[1]

---

1. This translates the variant reading of P23; other manuscripts (ℵ²

18 By his own desire he gave us birth by the message of truth
that we would be unique among all his creatures.

The poem begins with an image of God as pure light, then moves into agricultural imagery of "firstfruits." God's light gives birth to spiritual life.

The Tongue (3:2–12)

2 In many ways, we all make mistakes.
But the perfect man is the one who makes
no mistakes in his speech because he bridles
his entire being by controlling his tongue.

3 Horses' every move are guided
by the bits riders put in their mouths.
4 Large ships, so heavy it takes strong winds
to move them, are guided by a small rudder
wherever the pilot wants to take her.

5 The tongue, such a small member,
boasts such great accomplishments.
A small flame can blaze down an entire forest.
So can the fire of the tongue.

6 Of all our members, it alone inflicts a world of hurt,
ruining our entire being, igniting a destructive cycle
born in the flames of hell[2] itself.

A C) read "there is no variation or shadow of turning," and still others (ℵ B) read, "there is no variation which consists in the turning of the shadow." Whereas these manuscripts speak only of God's invariability, P23 speaks of God's invariability and timelessness (viz. time was told by the turning of the shadow on a sun dial). For more on this, see my book, *New Testament Text and Translation Commentary*, 724–725.

2. Greek, *Gehenna*, a place of fiery destruction.

7 Every species of beasts, birds, reptiles, and sea creatures
has been tamed by the human species.
8 But no one has been able to tame the human tongue,
for it is rebellious, evil, and full of deadly poison.

9 With the same tongue, we bless our Lord and Father
and curse people who are made in his likeness.
10 Oh, how can it be that both blessing and cursing
flow from the same mouth! This shouldn't be—
11 fresh and brackish water don't spring from the same
    opening.
12 And just as fig trees can't produce olives and grapevine
    figs,
salt water will never yield fresh liquid for drink.

This poem reveals James' knowledge and use of a number of images current in his day. As for the second stanza, which speaks of the disproportionate power of the tongue, James used the image of a small bit controlling a horse and a rudder contolling a ship. In Sophocles' *Antigone* one of the actors says, "I know that spirited horses are broken by the use of a small bit" (477). Aristotle contrasted the small size of the rudder, operated by one man, with the huge mass of the ship it controls (*Queast. Mechan.* 5). In the fourth stanza, my translation "igniting a destructive cycle" is literally "igniting the cycle of life." The expression "cycle of life" (or "cycle of nature") was used "in the Orphic religion to describe the uneding cycle of reincarnations from which deliverance was sought. [This] philosophical expression had become popularized and was used in James' day as a way of describing the course of human life, perhaps with an emphasis on the 'ups and downs' of life" (Moo, *James*, 125). The fourfold division of animals noted in the fifth stanza comes from Genesis 1:26;

the notion of the tongue being a deadly poison comes from OT verses like Psalm 140:3; Proverbs 10:8; 11:9. In stanza 6, the image of "like begets only like" (vines produce grapes, fig trees yield figs) is found in Epicetus' *Discourses* (2.18–20) and Jesus' Sermon on the Mount (Matt 7:16).

Spiritual Fidelity (4:4–10)

4 Adulteresses, don't you know that befriending the world makes you an enemy of God.
5 Don't you know what the Scriptures mean that say,
"God jealously desires that the spirit he placed within us would be for him"[3]—to these he gives abundant grace,
6 *for God opposes the proud and graces the humble.*[4]
7 Submit to God, oppose the devil, and he will flee from you.
8 Draw near to God, and he will draw near to you.
Cleanse your hands, you sinners,
and purify your hearts, you double-minded.
9 Lament, mourn, and weep.
Let your laughter turn to mourning and your joy to gloom.
10 Humble yourself before the Lord and he will exalt you.

James' condemnation is steeped in the poetic language of the OT prophets who viewed the relationsip between God and his people as a marriage, and consequently any violation thereof as adultery (see Isa 54:1–6; Jer 2:2; 3:20; Hos 2:5–20). This sanctity of the marriage is emphasized in the statement that "God jealously desires that the spirit he placed within us would be for him," a statement that can't be found in any OT verse—though the idea of God's jealousy for his people

3. The source of this citation is unknown.
4. The citation comes from the Greek version of Proverbs 3:34.

is found in verses such as Exodus 20:5; 34:14; Zechariah 8:2. The second part of the poem fleshes out James' idea of what it means to humble oneself before God, the verse quoted in Proverbs 3:34.

Warnings to the Rich (5:1–6)

1 Oh, you rich people, weep and howl
for the miseries that will befall you,
2 as all your wealth rots
and your clothes get eaten by moths.

3 Your gold and silver have corroded—
the rust is God's verdict against you,
as it devours your flesh like fire.
How foolish to store treasures for the last day!

4 The wages you withheld from those
who mowed your fields cry out against you!
The moans of the harvesters you cheated
reach the ears of the Lord of heaven's forces.

5 You lived on earth in luxury and pleasure,
unaware you were fattening yourselves for slaughter.
6 You condemned and murdered the Righteous One
who now stands in judgment against you.

The first two stanzas of this poem reflect the same kind of poetic imagery Jesus used to depict the evanasence of wealth (see Matt 6:19–20; Luke 6:24). The last two stanzas could have come out of the mouth of any OT prophet who decried wealthy people's exploitation of the poor souls who slaved to make them rich (see Amos 2:6–7; 5:12; Micah 3:1–3).

The image of fattening themelves for their own slaughter is original and powerful. Though it was people like them who killed the Righteous One, Jesus Christ (see NLT mg), they would have to face his judgment on the day of the Lord.

Patience for the Lord's Parousia (5:7–8)

> 7 Wait patiently for the Lord's parousia,
> as the farmer waits early and late rains
> to ripen earth's precious grains.
> 8 As you wait patiently, stay encouraged,
> for the Lord's parousia has come near.

This short poem, which is arranged chiastically (A B C B' A'), draws upon imagery that was well known to the agricultural society of Palestine, where the autumn rain comes in October and November soon after the grain is sown, while the spring rain comes in March and April prior to the harvest (see Deut 11:14; Jer 5:24; Hosea 6:3; Joel 2:24).

9

The First Epistle of Peter

Christ, the Regenerator (1:23–25)

23 We have been regenerated
    not with seed that decomposes,
24 as to that which the Scripture says—
    all humans are as wild flowers
    whose glory comes with summer bloom,
    but whose petals dry and blossoms fall—
25 no, we have been conceived by the Lord's
imperishable word to flourish amaranthine.

The poem, craftfully built around Isaiah 40:6–8, celebrates regeneration by the Lord's word through the poetic image of seed and flower; it compares the natural process of decay with the spiritual reality of non-decay.

Christ, the Cornerstone (2:4–10)

4 Rejected by men, he is God's chosen;
    his precious One became the living Stone,
5 to whom we come and by whom we are built
    into a spiritual house, a sacred priesthood
presenting spiritual sacrifices that God accepts
    because we belong to Jesus Christ.

6 This stands written in the Scriptures:

In Zion I place a cornerstone
  who is the precious, chosen One.
Whoever places their trust in him
  will never be dismayed.[1]

7 To you who believe he is precious,
  but not to those who don't believe.

The cornerstone chosen for God's building
  had been rejected by the builders.[2]
8 *They stumbled over the stone,*
  they tripped over the rock
because they didn't see the chosen One of God.
  This was their destiny.[3]

9 But you, who have seen his marvelous light,
  are a chosen people, a royal priesthood,
  a sacred nation, God's precious treasure.

You have been called out of your darkness
  to express his awesome gloriousness.
10 *You, who once were not a people,*
  are now the people of God.
You, who once lived without mercy,
  are now mercifully blessed.[4]

---

1. The citation comes from the Greek version of Isaiah 28:16.
2. The citation comes from Psalm 118:22.
3. The citation comes from Isaiah 8:14.
4. The citation comes from Hosea 1:6, 9; 2:23.

This poem is a textured collage of OT selections, which pronounce the national Jewish rejection of Jesus and celebrate the Gentile's acceptance of him and God's marvelous acceptance of him. The first three stanzas are sustained by the image of Christ as the precious cornerstone for God's new building, the church—a stone rejected by the Jewish leaders but chosen by God. All those who put their faith in him are incorporated into that living building, which is also a royal priesthood. This is beautifully expressed by the poet in the fourth stanza, who then selected the poetry of Hosea (in the fifth stanza) to cap off the theme of God accepting a brand new people to be his own.

Christ, the Suffering Healer (2:21–25)

21 You have been called to suffering
    because Christ also suffered[5] for you,
leaving you a path[6] to follow in the steps of him
    22 *who never commited a sin or spoke a lie,*[7]
    23 who didn't retaliate when he was reviled;
    who didn't strike back, when he was hit.
24 Rather, he committed himself to the righteous Judge
    when he took our sins to the tree
    and healed us with the wounds inflicted on his body.

---

5. Several ancient manuscripts (P72 A B C P 33) read "suffered," whereas others (P81 ℵ Ψ) read "died."

6. The Greek word for "path" is *hupogrammon*, which was used in teaching settings as an alphabetic exemplar leaving space under each letter for the student to copy. I wanted to use vocabulary that expresses this, such as "leaving you an example"—but the following image ("to follow in his steps") forces a word like "path." One way to keep both images is to translate it as "leaving you an example. Follow in his steps . . . ."

7. The citation comes from Isaiah 53:9.

> 25 Now we can die to sin and live right with God,
> no longer straying from our Shepherd
> but staying close to the Sentinel of our souls.

The poem holds together by the image of believers following Jesus' path of suffering with an allusion to how Jesus handled his trial and crucifixion. Then the "treed" Jesus becomes a symbol of his death giving life and healing. Then the imagery shifts to a risen Savior leading his sheep on the same path of suffering.

10

The First Epistle of John

John's first Epistle, with its spiraling repetition of themes, is symphonic. It is worthy of being read as poetry. (The New Jerusalem Bible presents the entire epistle as a poem.) The following arrangement, which differs from that of the New Jerusalem Bible, demonstrates this spiraling repetition: with the pattern of A B C, A B C, B C A.

> Prologue (1:1–4)
> A1. Living Righteously in Light & Truth (1:5–2:6)
> B1. Living in Light & Love (2:7–17)
> C1. Knowing False Teaching & True (2:18–27)
> A2. Living Righteously in the Truth (2:28–3:10)
> B2. Living in Love (3:11–24)
> C2. Knowing False Teaching & True (4:1–6)
> B3. Living in Love (4:7–5:4)
> C3. Knowing False Teaching & True (5:5–13)
> A3. Living Righteously in the Truth (5:14–21)

The careful reader will realize that John's encyclical epistle has the same vocabulary as in his Gospel; the difference is that in the epistle the words and phrases are terser, repeated with greater variation, and are somewhat more mysterious (because the expressions do not appear in the kind of contexts one finds in John's Gospel). As with the Gospel, the epistle is both deceptively simple and intriguingly deep. It makes for profound poetry and thoughtful reading.

Prologue (1:1–4)

> 1 As to what was from the beginning
> > what we have heard
> > what we have seen with our eyes
> > what we have gazed upon
> > and as to what we have touched—
> > this is the Word of Life.
>
> 2 For the Life was manifested
> > to us who have seen him
> > and now give living witness
> > as we proclaim to you
> > the eternal Life who was with Father
> > and was revealed to us.
>
> 3 What we have seen and heard
> > we proclaim to you
> > so that you may join
> > our sacred fellowship
> > in communion with the Father
> > and with his Son, Christ Jesus.
>
> 4 This will give us all great joy.

Living Righteously in Light and Truth (1:5–2:6)

> 5 This is the message we heard from him
> and proclaim to you: "God himself is light;
> in him there is no shade of darkness."

6 If we claim to be in communion with him
and at the same time move in darkness
we are living a lie, not even close to truth.

7 But if we live where he lives--in the light—
we will enjoy communion with each other,
knowing that the blood of his Son, Jesus,
keeps us clean from every sin.

8 If we claim, "I don't have any sin,"
we are self-deceived and don't know the truth.
9 But if we confess our sins, he is faithful and just
to forgive us and cleanse us from unrighteousness.
10 Yes, if we claim, "I haven't sinned,"
we not only make him a liar, we make it clear
that his word isn't alive in our lives.

Chapter Two

1 My dear children,
this writing should encourage you not to sin.
2 But if anyone sins, we have an Arbiter,
the righteous Jesus Christ, standing before the Father
to make expiation for our sins—and not only ours
but the sins of the entire world.

3 If we heed what he has told us,
we know for certain that we know him.
4 Those who claim, "I know him,"
yet don't keep what the Lord has said,
are liars who don't know what is real.

5 Those who obey what he has said
are the ones who have perfect love for God.
By this we can be certain that we live in him.

6 Those who claim, "I abide in him,"
ought to live as Jesus lived.

Living in Light and Love (2:7–17)

7 My beloved friends,
I am not writing a new command for you
but one I told you long ago—
when I was first with you
and you heard my message.

8 Now I am writing a new command
because what is real in Jesus is also in you.
The darkness is passing away
as it's swallowed by illumination.
And the true light is already shining!

9 Those who claim, "I am in the light,"
but hate their brother or sister,
are still living in darkness.
10 Those who love their brother and sister
are living in the light and will not stumble.
11 Those who hate walk in darkness
and have no idea where they're headed
because the darkness has them blinded.

12 Children,
I am writing to you because you have been forgiven
of your sins in the Name of Jesus.
13 Fathers,
I am writing to you because you have known
the One who is from the beginning.
Young men,
I am writing to you because you have overcome
the evil one.

14 Children,
I write to you because you have known
the Father.
Fathers,
I write to you because you have known
the One who is from the beginning.
Young men,
I write to you because you are empowered
by the word of God living in you
to overcome the evil one.

15 Do not love the world
or the things the world offers.
Those who love the world
are void of love for the Father.

16 All that is present in this world—
the cravings of the flesh
the lust of the eyes
and the pride of possessions—
does not originate from the Father
but from what man has created.

17 This world is passing away,
and all its lust fading into nothing.
But those who live in God's ways
will remain until the everlasting age.

Knowing False Teaching and True (2:18–27)

18 Children,
the last hour is upon us.
You heard the Antichrist is coming.
Even now, many antichrists have come.
This is how we tell it is the last hour.

19 The ones who didn't belong among us
departed from our congregations.
Their departure shows that not one of them
20 was a true believer—you should know this
because you've been anointed by the sacred Spirit.

21 I am writing this to you because you know the truth,
and that no lie originates from truth.
22 Who is a liar but the one who denies that Jesus is the Christ?
The Antichrist is the liar because he denies the Father and Son.
23 Everyone who denies the Son doesn't know the Father;
everyone who confesses the Son knows the Father also.

24 Hold fast to what you heard from us in the beginning.
Keep it true among you and let it live in you.
25 Then you will always live in the Father and the Son,
who have given us the promise of living forever with them.

26 I am writing this concerning those who are deceiving you.
27 Since you have the anointing from the sacred One
living in you, I really don't need to teach you.
This anointing will teach you what is true and what is not.
Stay true to this teaching and you will remain in him.

Living Righteously in the Truth (2:28–3:10)

28 Even now, my children, keep living in him,
so that when he appears in his parousia
we will appear before him with confidence.

29 Since you know that he is righteous,
you should also know that everyone
born of him lives a righteous life.

Chapter 3

1 What extrordinary love the Father has given us
that we should be called children of God.
This is who we are, even though the world
doesn't recognize this, as it didn't recognize Jesus.

2 Beloved friends, we are now God's children,
waiting for the manifestation of what we will become,
knowing that when Jesus is manifested we will be like him,
and then we will see him as he really is!
3 All who treasure this hope purify themselves
to be as pure as Jesus is.

4 When we break God's law, we sin.
While we know that sin is lawlessness,
5 we also know that Jesus, who has no sin,
was manifested to take away every sin.

6 Everyone who continues to live in him
will not continue living in sin.
Everyone who keeps practicing sin
has not seen him or really known him.
7 Children, don't be deceived by anyone;
righteousness is practiced only by the righteous.
And Jesus is the righteous One.

8 Those who practice sin belong to the devil,
who has sinned ever since the beginning.
For this reason the Son of God was manifested:
to destroy the deeds of the devil.

9 Those who have been born of God
cannot keep sinning because God's seed

lives in them—and God's life enables them
to live a life free from constant sin.
10 This is how the children of God are manifested;
they are different from the children of the devil
who do not practice a righteous life
and have no love for others.

Living in Love (3:11–24)

11 This is the message you heard from us
in the beginning: "love your sisters and brothers."
12 Don't be like evil Cain who belonged to the evil one
and murdered his brother because he was righteous.
13 And don't wonder why the world hates you.

14 We know we have migrated from death to life
because we love our brothers and sisters;
15 those who don't love have stayed in death.
Their hatred has made them murderers,
none of whom have eternal life living inside.

16 We have known what love really is—
we saw it when Jesus laid his life down for us.
We should do the same for our brothers.

17 Those who have wordly possessions
and close their hearts to those in need
could not have God's love alive in them.
18 My children, we shouldn't espouse love
then fail to show it's genuine in our lives.

19 Our love lets us know we are living in the truth;
this gives us confidence to be in his presence,
even when our hearts tend to condemn us.

20 God, who is greater than our feelings,
knows everything about our love or lack thereof.

21 Beloved friends, if our hearts don't condemn us,
we really have confidence to be in God's presence
22 and to receive whatever we ask him—
because we keep his commands
and live a life that pleases him.

23 And this is the command: that we trust
in the Name of his Son, Jesus Christ,
who told us to love one another.
24 Those who keep this, live in him and he in them.
And we know that he himself resides in us
because he gave us his very own Spirit.

Chapter 4

Knowing False Teaching and True (4:1–6)

1 Beloved friends,
don't believe the spirit of every prophet
but test their spirits to see if they're of God,
because many false prophets travel around.
2 We know that a prophet has the Spirit of God
if that prophet confesses Jesus Christ came in the flesh.
If not, their spirit is not God's;
3 even worse, their spirit is that of the Antichrist,
of whom you heard he is coming—
even now his spirit is already in the world.

4 Dear children,
since you belong to God, you are overcomers.
The one living in you is mightier
than the spirit living in this world.

5 Since these prophets belong to the world,
they speak the kind of things the world likes.
6 We who belong to God are heard
by those who really know him;
those who don't know God don't hear us.
By this we learn the difference
between those who have Spirit of truth
and those who have a spirit that's false.

Living in Love (4:7–5:4)

7–8 Beloved friends,
Because God is love, we should love one another.
Those who love are children of God who know him.
Those who don't love don't really know him.

9 God's love was manifested among us in his only Son
who was sent into this world for us to live in him.
10 Love for God did not originate from us;
rather, he loved us and gave us his Son
to sacrifice his life to take away our sins.

11 Beloved friends,
if God loved us so, we should love one another.
12 None of us has ever seen God,
but he is manifest in us when we love,
especially as our love grows toward perfection.

13 We know that we reside in him and he in us
because he has given us his Spirit.
14 We are the ones who saw Jesus and testify
that he is the Son of God sent by the Father
to be the Savior of the world.
15 Those who confess that Jesus is God's Son
have God living in them and they in God.

16 We have known and believed that God loves us.
Since God is love, those who live in love live in God,
    and God lives in them.
17 When love reaches its perfection in us
we can be confident in the day of judgment—
because even while living in this world
we have become like Jesus.
18 Love and fear are incompatible.
When love is perfected, fear is negated
and we no longer dread punishment.
Those who live in fear have not perfected love.

19 We love because God first loved us.
Anyone who claims, "I love God,"
but hates his brother is simply a liar.
20 How can you love God whom you haven't seen
when you don't love the brother you can see?
21 Remember, this was his command:
those who love God must love their brothers.

Chapter Five

1 Those who believe that Jesus is the Christ
have been born of God and will love
all others who have also been born of him.
2–3 By this we know that we love the children of God:
when we love God and keep his commands—
4 and they are not overbearing because the life
we have from God overcomes the world.
Our faith in him gives us the victory.

Knowing False Teaching and True (5:5–13)

5 Those who overcome the spirit of the world
are those who believe that Jesus is God's Son.

6 Jesus Christ showed himself to be God's Son
through baptism's water and his blood on the cross.
He was God's Son in baptism and crucifixion.
The Spirit of truth testifies to this reality.
7 There are three who give one testimony:
8 the Spirit, the water, and the blood.

9 If we trust the testimony of men,
we should realize that God's testimony
concerning his Son is much greater.
10 Those who believe in the Son of God
have the witness in their spirits.
Those who do not believe make God a liar
because they reject God's testimony about his Son.

11 This is the testimony:
God has given us eternal life,
and this divine, eternal life is in his Son.
12 Those who have the Son have this life;
those who don't have God's Son
do not have eternal life.

13 I wrote to you so that you may know
that you have eternal life
because you have believed the Son of God.

Living Righteously in the Truth (5:14–21)

14 This is the confidence we possess
when we approach God—that if we ask
anything according to his will, he hears us.
15 If we know that he hears us when we ask,
then we know that he will answer our requests.

16 If anyone sees a brother committing a sin
that does not lead to death, he can ask God
who will give him life, because his sin isn't mortal.
I do not say that you should pray for mortal sins.
17 Of course, every unrighteous act is sin,
But I am speaking about the sin that leads to death.

18 We know that everyone who has been born of God
does not continually sin because the Only One,
God's Son, protects him from the evil one.
19 We know that we belong to God,
while the whole world is held by the evil one.
20 And we know that the Son of God has come
and given us spiritual understanding
so that we may know the true One
and live in the true One, his Son, Jesus Christ
who is the true God and eternal life.

21 Dear children,
protect yourselves from what replaces God,
for that is idolatry.

11

The Epistle of Jude

Doxology to Savior God and Jesus Christ (Jude 24–25)

Praise him who has the power
> to keep you from falling
> to make you blameless
> and to give you good standing
in his glorious presence!

Praise the one and only God, our Savior,
> who does all this through Jesus Christ.
To him be glory, majesty, dominion, and power
> before all time and now and forever!

This doxology displays Jude's poetic power as he praises God the Savior through Jesus Christ for his ability to protect the believer, purify the believer, and uphold the believer—by the power of glorious presence.

12

The Book of Revelation

Prologue Poem to Jesus Christ's Revelation (1:1–8)

1–2 This is Jesus Christ's revelation,
    which God unveiled to him.
What Jesus saw he showed to his servants
    and told them what was coming quickly.
He made it known by sending his angel to John,
    his servant, who recorded God's message
    and the testimony of Jesus Christ.

3 Blessings to the one who reads this book aloud
    and to those who hear the message
of this prophecy and adhere to what is written,
    for the time of fulfillment is near.

4 John blessed the seven churches in Asia, saying:
    Grace to you and peace from the One
    Who Is and Who Was and Who Is To Come,
    from the seven Spirits before his throne,
    5 and from Jesus Christ, the faithful martyr,
    firstborn of the dead, ruler of every earthly king.
6 Because of his love he shed his blood for us, freeing us
    from our sins,
and he made us a kingdom of priests to serve his father God.
    All glory and dominion to him forever!

> 7 Look! He is coming with the clouds
>   so that every eye will see him,
>   even those who pierced him.
>   All the tribes of the earth will wail.
>
> 8 For he is the Lord God who says,
> "I am the Alpha and the Omega, the Almighty One,
> Who Is and Who Was and Who Is To Come."

As with other prologue poems in John's writings (see John 1:1–18; 1 John 1:1–4), this proem is artfully written. Not only is it a moving piece of literature in and of itself (note the sudden shift in speakers and viewpoints), it functions to provide a poetic introduction to some of the major themes of the book, especially the revelation of Jesus Christ, "the faithful martyr, firstborn of the dead, ruler of every earthly king" whose purpose is to establish "a kingdom of priests to serve his father God."

Vision of the Son of Man (1:12–16)

12–13 When I turned to see the voice speaking to me,
I saw one like the Son of Man standing
between seven lampstands
clothed with a priestly robe
tied around his chest with a golden sash:
14 his hair is white like wool,
his eyes ignited as with fire,
15 his feet like burnished bronze glowing in a furnace,
his voice as the sound of roaring surf,
16 his hand holding seven stars,
his mouth a two-edged flashing sword,
his face effulgent as in full sun's strength.

This passage is poetic by virtue of the the number of similes John used to describe the person he saw standing in the midst of the seven lampstands.

The Living Adytum (4:2–11)

2 I was enlivened in spirit
    and envisioned in the Adytum
3 One seated on a throne who shone
    like jasper and carnelian stone
    circled by an emerald rainbow.

4 Around the throne were twenty four more
    in which were seated elders in white robes
    with golden diadems on their heads.

5–6 Flashes of lightning ignited the Adytum
    with rumbling and pealing thunder.
In front of throne I saw a glassy sea
    as clear as crystal refecting the flaming light
    of seven burning torches, which are God's seven Spirits.

7 Four Zoa, the cherubim, surround the throne,
    full of eyes front and behind.
The first Zoa looks lion, the second Zoa ox,
the third Zoa countenances a human face,
the fourth Zoa an eagle in flight—
    8 each have six wings and many eyes
    within their translucent beings.

Day and night the Zoa unceasingly chant:
    Sacred, sacred, sacred is the Lord God Almighty
    who Was and Is and Is To Come!

9 As the Zoa give glory, honor, and praise
to the enthroned One, who lives forever,
10 the twenty four elders sitting before him
prostrate themselves before the One living forever
    and throw their diadems before the throne, saying:

> 11 *O Lord our God, you are worthy of glory,*
> *esteem, and power, for you create everything.*
> *Because of your desire they existed before*
> *they were and became what they are now!*

This passage contains two kinds of poems: the first is that of the visionary attempting to explain what he sees and hears by using simile and metaphor; the second is that of the chants (or hymns) he heard in the adytum (4:8, 11).

Worthy to Open the Apocalyptic Pages (5:1–13)

1 The enthroned One held a book in his hand
    with writing inside and on the back.
I could see that it was sealed with seven seals,
2 and I saw a mighty angel proclaim with loud voice,
"Who is worthy to break the seals and open the book?"

3 But no one in heaven, on earth, or under earth
was found worthy enough to break the seals,
    to open the pages, and look inside the book.
4 I wept greatly because of this—
until I heard the voice of one proclaim:
5 *"Don't weep. Can't you see Judah's Lion!*
David's Scion has ascended the heavenly Adytum,
taking his place between the throne, Zoa, and elders!"

6 I saw him enthroned between the Zoa and elders.
He looked like a slain Lamb
with seven horns and seven eyes,
which are the seven Spirits of God
dispersed to every corner of earth!

7 And when he took the book from God's hand,
the four living Zoa and twenty four elders
prostrated themselves before the Lamb.

8 Playing harps and swinging incense bowls,
    which are the prayers of saints,
they began to sing this new song:

9 *You are worthy to open the apocalyptic pages*
because you purchased the people of God
    with your very blood—
10 *people from every tribe, tongue, and nation,*
    and you made them a kingdom of priests
serving our God, destined to reign on earth.

11 Then I saw—no, heard the voice of angels, Zoa,
    and elders resound from the Adytum--
12 the voice of myriads and myriads,
    thousands and thousands, proclaiming
    as loud as ocean roar:

Worthy is the slain Lamb to be given
all power, wealth, wisdom, and strength;
all honor, glory, and praise!

13 Then I heard every living creature—
    celestial, terrestial, subterranean, cetacean—
adulating the enthroned One and the Lamb:

> *All praise, honor, glory, and dominion*
> *are yours forever into eternal ages.*
>
> 14 "Amen!" proclaimed the four Zoa
> and the elders, who fell prostrate before
> the God they worship and adore.

This passage is poetic in two ways: first, the poet exhibits the visionary's expression of what he was seeing and hearing through the use of metaphor; second it contains the hymns of those in the adytum (5:9–10, 12–13).

Praise to Jesus, the Lamb (7:9–12, 14–17)

9 I saw a multitude no one could count,
>   from every nation, tribe, people, and tongue
> standing before the throne and the Lamb.

Robed in white, with palm fonds in their hands,
>   10 they lifted loud adulation:
> *Salvation comes from the enthroned One;*
>   *rescue comes from the Lamb!*

11 All the angels encircling the throne,
>   the elders, and four living Zoa
> prostrated themselves before their God
>   whom they extoled:

12 *Amen! All praise, glory, thanksgiving, wisdom,*
honor, power, and strength belongs to our God
into the eternal ages. Amen!

14 Then I saw another multitude of those
>   who had risen from terrible tribulation
> and had whitened their robes in the Lamb's blood.

15 They stand before the throne of God worshiping him
   within his sanctuary, without ceasing day and night.
The enthroned One shelters them with his presence
   like a tent spread over their heads,
   16 *so they won't be struck by the sun's scorching rays.*
   They will never hunger or thirst[1]
17 because the enthroned Lamb will shepherd them,
   guiding them to springs of living water—
   and God will wipe away every tear from their eyes.

This passage is poetic in two ways: it contains two short hymns of exaltation (7:10, 12), which are then followed by a pastoral description of the eternal bliss enjoyed by God's people (7:14–17), modeled after verses like Psalm 23:1–2; Isaiah 25:8; 49:10; Jeremiah 31:16.

Praise to the King (11:15–18)

15 After the seventh angel sounded his trumpet,
I heard loud voices in heaven proclaiming:

The kingdom of the world has become the Lord's dominion—
his Messiah will rule his kingdom forever and ever!

16 The twenty-four enthroned elders
fell prostrate before him and worshiped God:

17 *We thank you, Lord God, Almighty,*
   the One who Is and who Was,
because you have exerted great power
   to begin your dominion
   and destroy those who destroyed earth.

---

1. The citation comes from Isaiah 49:10.

> 18 *As the nations raged, your anger fumed*
> > *until the time came for you to judge the dead*
> *and reward your servants—*
> > *the prophets, the saints, and all who revere your Name,*
> > *whether they had fame or not.*

This passage, which is presented as a poem in *Novum Testamentum Graece* (27th edition), is essentially a victory hymn celebrating the divine King's reign over the nations of the world. Modeled after Psalm 2, the poem extols the fact that the Lord God has appointed his Messiah (the Christ) to rule the world (cf. Acts 4:26–28). Verse 15, coming in the middle of the book of Revelation, is climatic: "The kingdom of the world has become the Lord's dominion—his Messiah will rule his kingdom forever and ever!" What the prophets anticipated is proclaimed as now realized (Dan 2:31–45; Zech 14:9).

Satan's Demise, Christ's Reign Begins (12:1–12)

1 An awful augur appeared in heaven:
a woman draped in sun,
crowned with twelve stars, standing on the moon,
2 agonizing in awful labor, ready to deliver.

3 And yet another sign appeared in heaven:
a fiery dragon with seven diademed heads, ten horns,
4 and tail sweeping away many stars from heaven.
He hung hungry over the woman, poised to pounce
and devour her child as soon as he was born.

5 But the child born to shepherd all nations
and rule them with an iron rod

was snatched up to the enthroned God
before the dragon had a chance to get him.

6 The woman fled into the wilderness
to a place prepared by God
for three and a half years of nourishment.

7 And then there was a war in heaven:
mighty Michael with his angels
battled the Dragon and his angelic forces,
8 forcing them out of the Adytum,
casting down the great Dragon,
9 known forever as the ancient Serpent,
the Devil and Satan, the deceiver of all mankind.

10 Then I heard heaven's voice proclaiming:

"Now begins the salvation and mighty kingdom
of our God and the Messiah's dominion
because the accuser of our comrades has been thrown down—
the one who accused them before God day and night.
11 But they overpowered him with the Lamb's blood,
for whom they all were martyred,
having loved him more than themselves.

12 What joy for those who've made heaven their home!
What sorrow awaits the earth and the sea
because the Devil has come down with awful fury
knowing his time in this world is about to end!

Although I have presented this entire passage as a poem, only verses 10–12 are distinctly poetic (so *Novum Testamentum Graece*, 27th edition). But I found it strange to separate the poem from ints narrative context; hence, I rendered the entire passage poetically.

The Song of Moses and the Lamb (15:2–4)

2 I saw a host of people who had overcome the beast
    standing on what looked like a sea on fire.
3 They played God's harps and sang the song of Moses,
    God's servant; then they sang the song of the Lamb:

Lord God, the Almighty One,
what you have done is powerful and awesome!
Your ways are true and just,
O King of the ages![2]

4 Who would not revere you, Lord,
    and glorify your Name?
All nations will come to worship you
who alone are the sacred One,
    more righteous than anyone.

Revelation 15:3–4 is "a lyric outburst on the greatness of God" (Barclay, *The Revelation of John* vol. 2, 120). Although some exegetes see this as one combined hymn, according to the Greek grammar and the syntax, it seems two songs were sung: Moses' song (which may not be recorded here) and then the Lamb's (which is presented in 15:3–4). If John intended the reader to see a combined song here, we should see it as a hymn celebrating God's deliverance of his people beginning with Moses and ending with Jesus, the Lamb (cf. Exod 15 with Rev 15). The hymn is filled with citations from the OT. The first stanza is taken from Psalm 111:3; Amos

---

2. Although it could be argued that the expression "king of the ages [*aionon*]" was borrowed from 1 Timothy 1:17, it has the impressive support of P47 ℵ*,2 C. Other manuscripts (ℵ¹ A 052 Maj) read "king of the nations [*ethnon*]"; this reading appears to be the result of scribal ameliorization to the next verse, which speaks of the "nations" fearing God.

3:13; 4:13; Deuteronomy 32:4. The phrase "king of the nations" (see alternative reading in note above) is found in Jeremiah 10:7, while the phrase "King of the ages" is found in 1 Enoch 9:4; 12:3; 25:3–7. The final stanza echoes Exodus 15:11 and Psalm 86:9.

Proclamations after the Third Bowl (16:4–7)

4 After the third angel poured out his bowl
into the rivers and springs, they became blood.
5 And I heard the angel over the waters proclaim:

You are just, the One Who Is and the One Who Was,
the sacred One, because you have executed judgment.
6 Those who shed the blood of saints and prophets
deserve to drink the bloody waters!
7 And I heard the altar reply,
Yes, Lord God, the Almighty,
your judgments are true and just.

Verses 5–7, which are set as a poem in *Novum Testamentum Graece* (27th edition), display a hymn that echoes the previous hymn (15:2–4). In both hymns, God is lauded as "the sacred One" and the "Lord God, the Almighty," whose judgments against the godless nations are true and just.

The Judgment of Babylon (18:1–10, 15–24)

1 After this I saw another angel coming down from heaven,
who had such magnificent power
that the earth was illuminated by his splendor.
2 He called out with a mighty voice:

> *The great Babylon has fallen! fallen!*
> *It has become a haunt of demons,*
> *a hideout of foul spirits, wicked birds,*
> *and prison of detestable creatures.*
>
> 3 *The nations have fallen with her*
> *because they drank the wine*
> *of her passionate, immoral sexuality--*
> *also the kings all over earth who slept with her,*
> *as well as the merchants who became rich*
> *by partaking of her luxurious wealth.*
>
> 4 And I heard another voice from heaven saying,
> *Come out of her, my people,*
> *so you don't get caught in their sins*
> *and have to share her plagues.*
>
> 5 *Her sins have piled up as high as heaven,*
> *reminding God of her unrighteousness.*
> *He will do to her as she did to others*
> 6 *and he will double his penalty for her evil,*
> *mixing a double portion in her cup.*
> *As much as she glorified herself by living luxuriously*
> *is as much as God will give her grief and torment.*
>
> 7 *Her heart was full of such thoughts as*
> *"I rule as a queen on my throne.*
> *I am not a widow. I'll never know pain."*
> 8 *Because of her pride, God will plague her*
> *with famine, death, and grief—all in one day.*
> *And she will be burned with fire*
> *by the mighty Lord God who judges her.*

*9 When the kings of earth, who slept with her
and lived in luxury with her, see her burning up in smoke,
they will weep and wail, as will all those standing far away
in fear of the torment she was suffering. They all lament,
"Misery, misery to Bablyon, the great and mighty city.
In one hour your judgment came!"*

*10 The merchants who became rich from her stand far away
in fear of her torment. They weep and wail,
"Misery, misery to the great city,
who clothed herself with finest purple and scarlet linen
and adorned herself with gold, precious stones, and pearls.
In one hour all this wealth was desolated!"*

*11 The merchants of the earth will grieve
because no one will buy their cargo anymore—
12 cargo of gold, silver, jewels and pearls,
fine linen, purple, silk and scarlet,
scented woods, ivory, expensive wood,
bronze, iron, marble,
13 cinnamon, spice, incense, myrrh, frankincense,
wine, olive oil, choice flour and wheat,
cattle, sheep, horses, chariots, slaves.
14 The fruit you craved is gone;
all your luxuries and splendid things are lost to you,
never to be found again!*

*15 All the shipmasters, seafarers, sailors, and crews
stand far away and watch her burn up in smoke.
With fear and dread, they lament,
16 "Misery, misery to the great city,
who clothed herself with fine linen, purple, and scarlet,
who was gilded with gold, precious gems, and pearls.*

17 In one hour this great wealth was desolated!"
All the shipmasters, seafarers, sailors, sea-merchants
stood far away and 18 cried out, as they saw her burning up
 in smoke:
"Was there ever a city as great as this?!"

19 Throwing dust on their heads, they weep and wail,
"What city was ever as great as this?
Misery, misery to the great city,
whose wealth was transported over the seas.
In one hour all this wealth was desolated!"

20 Rejoice over her destruction,
heaven's saints, apostles, and prophets,
for God has judged her for your sakes!

21 Then a mighty angel took a huge millstone
and threw it into the sea, saying,

The great city Babylon will be thrown down
with such violence it will never be found again.
22 The music of harpists, singers, flutists, and trumpeters
 will never be heard in you again!
Craftsmen of every kind and trade
 will never work in you again!
The sounds of a mill
 will never be heard in you again!
23 The light of a lamp
 will never shine in you again!
The cheerful voices of bride and groom
 will never be heard in you again!

Your merchants were the magnates of the world.
All nations were once deceived by your sorcery.

> 24 *On your hands was found the blood of prophets,*
> *saints, and martyrs from all over the earth.*

This section, which is presented in poetic format in *Novum Testamentum Graece* (27th edition) and many modern English versions, is an extended lamentation for the fall of Babylon. It is a dirge lamenting the destruction of a great power or city-state, much as one sees in the OT lamentations for Tyre (Ezek 26–28; Isa 23:1–18), Babylon (Isa 13:19–22; 47:7–9; Jer 50–51), and Nineveh (Zeph 2:14–15; Nah 3). Revelation 18:9–19 is very similar to Ezekiel's lamentation over Tyre in chapter 27 (both Ezekiel and John list nearly the same commodities). Revelation 18:21–24 is a doom song much like we read in Jeremiah 51:59–64.

The Wedding of the Lamb (19:1–9)

> 1 After this I heard what sounded like
> a loud voice of a large crowd in heaven:
>
> *"Hallelujah!*
> *Praise our God for his salvation, glory, and power.*
> *2 He rightly judged the great harlot*
> *who corrupted the world with her immorality.*
> *He avenged on her the blood of his servants."*
>
> 3 And they cried out a second time,
>
> *"Hallelujah!*
> *The smoke of her destruction*
> *ascends forever and ever!"*

4 The twenty-four elders, and four Zoa
prostrated themselves before God on his throne
and worshiped him: *"Amen. Hallelujah!"*

5 Then a voice sounded from the throne:

Praise our God, all his servants
and those who revere him,
whether the well-known or unknown!

6 Then I heard the roar of a great crowd
like the roar of ocean waves breaking
and mighty thunder pealing, saying:

Hallelujah, the Lord our God, the Almighty reigns!
7 Let us rejoice and extol him, giving him glory
because the wedding of the Lamb has come—
8 his bride has prepared herself, dressed in fine linen
as pure and bright as the brilliant deeds of the saints.

9And he says to me, write this:
Blessings on those invited to the Lamb's wedding feast.
This is the promise of the trustworthy God.

This section contains several short expressions of thanksgiving, held together by the outburst of "Hallejuah" (which means "praise Jah"), occuring 4 times throughout the section (vv. 1, 3, 4, 6), and nowhere else in the NT. This "Hallelujah chorus," extolling God for his just judgments and praising him for wedding feast of the Lamb, provides a bridge between the destruction of Babylon and the presentation of the new Jerusalem, which is the bride of the Lamb.

New Heaven, New Earth, New Jerusalem (21:1–7; 22:1–5)

1 I saw a brand new heaven and earth—
the former earth, heaven, and sea were no more.
2 I saw the sacred city, new Jerusalem, descending from heaven
adorned as a beautiful bride for her husband.
3 I heard a loud voice from the throne proclaim:

God is living with his people and they with him.
He himself will always be with them—
Immanuel come to dwell with his people!
4 God will wipe every tear from their eyes,
and kill all pain, grief, and death.

5 All this will come to pass by the One
  who turns the past into something new,
6 for he is the Alpha through Omega,
  the Beginning to the very End.
7 Those who conquer will be his children.

Chapter 22

1 They will drink of the living waters flowing
  from the throne of the God-Man, Lamb divine.
2 They will eat everlasting fruit from the living Tree
  and be healed forever from all disease.
3 The illumined God beaming through the Lamb
  will be their light brighter than the sun.
4 They will see God's grace and goodness
  shining in the face of their beloved Jesus Christ.

I combined these two poetic sections together (21:1–7 and 22:1–4) because they present the same futuristic pastoral scene of the eternal bliss God's people will experience in the presence of God as embodied in Jesus Christ. The language is full of metaphors depicting the end of death's sadness and the beginning of life's well-spring of eternal health and joy! The tree of life, lost in Eden, is now available as incarnate in Jesus Christ.

Jesus' Final Words (22:12–13, 16–17, 20)

12 Look, I am coming soon,
bringing my rewards with me
to pay each and every one
according to what they've done.

13 I am the Alpha and Omega,
the First and the Last,
the Beginning to the very End.

16 It is I, Jesus, who sent my angel to John
with this revelation to the believers' gatherings.
17 I am the root and scion of David,
the brilliant star of morning's dawn.

The Spirit and the bride say, "come."
Let everyone who hears say, "come."
Let everyone who is thirsty come
and drink freely of the living water.

20 I am coming soon!

The last poetic portions of Revelation are found in Jesus' final statements, in which he identifies himself as "I am the Alpha and Omega,/the First and the Last,/the Beginning to the very End"—a refrain that has appeared in various forms throughout Revelation as pronounced by God and Jesus. Here, Jesus makes it very clear that he is the eternal God. This is underlined by his assertion that he is both David's root (i.e., the source of David) and David's scion (i.e., the descendant of David). This is in line with the argument Jesus used with the religious leaders to affirm his deity (see Matt 22:41–45).

Bibliography

Aland, K., et al. *Novum Testamentum Graece*, 27th edition. Stuttgart: Deutsche Bibelgesellschaft, 2001. (NT manuscript listings can be found in this volume.)

Barclay, William. *The Revelation of John*, 2 vols. Philadelphia: Westminster, 1959.

Bauer, W. *A Greek-English Lexicon of the New Testament and Other Early Christian Literature* (abbreviated as BAGD). Chicago: University of Chicago Press, 1979.

Bruce, F. F. *The Acts of the Apostles*. Grand Rapids, Eerdmans, 1990.

———. *The Epistles to the Colossians, to Philemon, and to the Ephesians.* Grand Rapids: Eerdmans, 1984.

Comfort, Philip. *New Testament Text and Translation Commentary*. Wheaton: Tyndale, 2008.

———. *Philippians*. Wheaton: Tyndale, 2008.

Comfort, Philip, and J. Driesbach. *The Many Gospels of Jesus*. Wheaton: Tyndale, 2008.

Comfort, Philip, and W. Hawley, *Opening John's Gospel and Epistles*. Wheaton: Tyndale, 2009.

Fee, Gordon. *Paul's Letter to the Philippians*. Grand Rapids: Eerdmans, 1995.

Hawthorne, Gerald. *Philippians*. Waco: Word, 1983.

Liddell, H., and R. Scott, *A Greek-English Lexicon*. Oxford: Clarendon Press, 1968.

Moo, Douglas. *James*. Leicester: InterVarsity Press, 2000.

Moulton, J., and G. Milligan, *The Vocabulary of the Greek New Testament*. Grand Rapids: Eerdmans, 1972.

O'Brien, Peter. *The Epistle to the Philippians*. Grand Rapids: Eerdmans, 1991.

Schnakenburg, R. *The Gospel according to St. John*, 3 vols. Translator, K. Smyth. New York: Crossroad, 1980.

Wood, A. "Ephesians" in *Expositor's Bible Commentary*. Grand Rapids: Zondervan, 1978.

www.ingramcontent.com/pod-product-compliance
Lightning Source LLC
Chambersburg PA
CBHW051104160426
43193CB00010B/1311